INFAMOUS ESSEX WOMEN

DEE GORDON

First published in the United Kingdom in 2009 by
The History Press
The Mill, Brimscombe Port,
Stroud, Gloucestershire, GL5 2QG
www.thehistorypress.co.uk

Reprinted 2012

Copyright © Dee Gordon, 2009

All rights reserved. No part of this publication may be reproduced, stored in a retrieval system, or transmitted, in any form or by any means, electronic, mechanical, photocopying, recording or otherwise, without the prior permission of the publisher and copyright holder.

Dee Gordon has asserted the moral right to be identified as the author of this work.

British Library Cataloguing in Publication Data
A catalogue record for this book is available from the British Library.

ISBN 978-07509-5085-5

Typeset in 10/13pt Sabon
Typesetting and origination by
The History Press.
Printed and bound in England.

Contents

Introduction . . . and not forgetting Boudicca	v
Maud de Ingelrica	1
Alice Perrers	4
Essex Witches	9
Elizabeth Blount	13
Mary Boleyn	16
Anne Boleyn	18
Mary I	21
Katherine Seymour	26
Elizabeth I	29
Thomasine Tyler	33
Frances Rich	35
Lady Penelope Rich	38
Frances Howard	44
Ann Carter	47
Margaret Cavendish	49
Abigail Masham	53
Catherine Canham	56
Elizabeth Jeffryes	59

Child Murderers	62
Mary Wollstonecraft	68
Anne Broadrick	70
Mary Anne Clarke	75
Lady Smugglers	79
Mary May	82
Sarah Chesham	85
Kitty O'Shea	89
Ellen Willmott	93
Frances Greville	97
Ladies of the Road	102
Amy Bull	106
Sylvia Pankhurst	108
Edith Thompson	113
Conclusion	118
Bibliography	119
Acknowledgements	122

Introduction . . .
and not forgetting Boudicca

Well-behaved women rarely make history, and this applies to Essex as to any other county. Admittedly, in recent times, Essex girls have been making the kind of embarrassing history that posterity could do without. But dig a little deeper and Essex history reveals other women, including members of the royal family and the landed gentry, who are infamous for a variety of reasons.

An interesting mixture is revealed in the following chapters. Eccentrics and elopers, mistresses and murderers, rebels and rioters, witches and . . . a warrior.

The warrior, however, although infamous in Essex, is not of Essex. This is, of course, Queen Boudicca. (or Boadicea – meaning victory). She was Queen of the Iceni, a tribe covering most of what is now East Anglia: Norfolk, North Suffolk and North-East Cambridgeshire, but excluding Essex. However, her reputation in Essex is such that she could hardly be excluded from a book about its infamous women.

She has been described (by Dio Cassius – a Roman historian writing over a century later), as tall, fierce, and harsh-voiced with a great mass of 'the tawniest hair'. (Her red hair, incidentally, would have represented high status, but it also represented the different, and in the middle ages came to represent witchcraft.) Little is known of her

Statue of Boudicca, Thames Embankment. (Author's Collection)

Ambresbury Banks, Epping Forest. (Author's Collection)

origins. She would probably have been in her thirties when the Romans annexed the land belonging to the Iceni following the death of her husband, King Prasutagus. They also called in loans and attempted to levy additional taxes, reneging on the promises they had made to the Iceni King. The Romans flogged Boudicca to try to silence her protests, and violated her two teenage daughters.

Of course, this did not have the desired result and, in about 61 AD, Boudicca roused neighbouring tribes until she had an army of at least 20,000 (some quote as many as 100,000 or more). Her wild army overwhelmed the Roman settlement at Colchester, leaving just a thin layer of ash behind; they moved on to burn London (a twenty-year-old settlement) and destroyed Verulamium, near modern-day St Albans, in spite of their lack of arms and preparation. Boudicca's Britons carried out bestial atrocities – cutting off the breasts of noble women and sewing them to their mouths to make it look as if they were eating them is just one horrifying example, although allowances have to be made for exaggeration of contemporary reports, especially by Romans.

Tennyson may have described her as a heroine, but primarily Boudicca was a savage warrior, whatever allowances can be made for her motivation. About 70,000 people were killed before the Romans were able to defeat Boudicca and her Britons, wiping out the Icenis. The location of their final defeat is the subject of historic debate, but it is unlikely to have been Essex.

The details of her death are lost in the annals of ancient history. She may have taken poison after a last stand at Ambresbury Banks in Epping Forest – or maybe not. She may have also poisoned her daughters – or again, maybe not. She may be buried at Bartlow Hills (a burial ground formerly in Essex, now just over the border in Cambridgeshire), or under a platform at King's Cross Station (a possible battle site) – who knows?

Boudicca may have been the first of many feisty women linked with Essex, but she was certainly not the last. The stories that follow are in chronological order, up to and including the twentieth century.

Maud De Ingelrica

c. 1032–c. 1083

Ingelrica was the daughter of Ingelric, an Anglo-Saxon nobleman. Her father was the benefactor of the collegiate church of St Martin-le-Grand in London, where she was born. He was reputedly one of the wealthiest, if not the wealthiest, man in all of England at the time. One of his ancestors was said to be Joseph of Arimathea who surfaced in England after the death of Jesus, and a golden cross was used as a device by the family as a result. As to the female line of descent, unfortunately this can only be guesswork.

It seems that her son, William, was born in about 1050, some ten years before she married Ranulph Peverel. If Ingelrica had met William the Conqueror at the time he visited her father, recorded in 1049 when William was in his early twenties and she seventeen, then the stories of their mutual attraction could certainly have resulted in the birth of a child. Legend has it that both were striking figures, tall and charismatic, and the attraction would have been perfectly understandable.

William, or Guillaume, was betrothed to his cousin, Matilda of Flanders, at the time, and returned to France to do his duty, cementing the English-French alliance. But it appears he returned after the birth of William, seeming to confirm his reputed fatherhood of the boy. There is conjecture that Ingelrica and William were actually married in a ceremony at 'the ancient Temple church of London'.

So was she his mistress? Probably. Was William the Conqueror guilty of bigamy when he married Matilda in about 1053? Possibly. It is interesting to speculate that gossip surrounding the birth of the Conqueror's son was one of the reasons that delayed the Pope's agreement to William's marriage to Matilda. But if the Pope knew about the baby, surely he could not have known about the marriage?

Once William/Guillaume was back on French soil, Ingelrica married Ranulph in about 1058 (another Norman) in Hatfield, now Hatfield Peverel, although they would have spent time in France. The Conqueror seems to have been reunited with his son at the Battle of Hastings, because young William is alleged to have been actively involved – on the side of the Normans. Just to confuse the issue, however, by 1066 Matilda also had a son named William, who would have been ten years old, so deciding on which William was which after nearly 1,000 years is a bit tricky. After the conquest,

The Peverel coat of arms. (Courtesy of Marjorie Gisi and Dale Updike/ http://freepages.genealogy.rootsweb.com)

The Priory, Hatfield Peverel. (Author's Collection)

The interior of St Andrew's church, Hatfield Peverel. (Author's Collection)

Ingelrica's son, William, who had taken the name Peverel from Ranulph, was greatly honoured by his royal father, receiving over a hundred holdings of land and property in central England, 162 in all as listed by 1086.

Ingelrica and Ranulph had other sons, at least one of whom, Ranulph junior, was also well favoured by the Conqueror. There was also a daughter, Emma; all the children born in Cambridgeshire between 1060 and 1069.

It would have been regarded as a good way to atone for her 'sins' for Ingelrica to found a college for secular canons, and that is exactly what she did. It was sited on high ground east of the River Ter, on what is now the main A12 from London to Colchester, and later converted to a Benedictine priory by William junior, subsequently dissolved by Henry VIII in 1538. The parish church of St Andrew's is the only surviving fragment of the Norman priory church nave.

The Peverel (Anglicised from Peuerel, meaning fearless) wealth has been the object of many stories of jealousy, animosity and concealment. Allegations of a cover-up of the Peverel connection with William the Conqueror have been well documented. The true story will now never be known.

Ingelrica, her reputation perhaps restored, and Ranulph, both died in Hatfield, the dates varying depending on the source. He seems to have been just a couple of years her senior, but it looks as if she survived him by a decade or so. An incomplete story full of theories but no less fascinating for all that.

Alice Perrers

c. 1330–c. 1400

Alice was described by a contemporary chronicler, Thomas Walsingham, a monk of St Albans, as a domestic drudge and as the daughter of a tiler from 'Henney' in Essex. There has since been speculation as to the truth of this claim – for instance, if Walsingham felt it appropriate to criticise Alice, then it would have been a good idea to suggest she was a) base born and b) the daughter of someone with the same occupation as the leader of the Peasants' Revolt during her lifetime (Wat Tyler). However, the two medieval hamlets of Great Henny and Little Henny, near Castle Hedingham, did have clay sites producing tiles for local houses at the time, so there could be truth in his version of events.

One difficulty in accepting such humble beginnings for Alice is to then accept that she was later engaged in royal service, almost impossible for someone with such an unprepossessing start in life. There was a more middle-class family of Perrers from Hertfordshire, and this could have been where Alice's roots lie, but it is also significant that in later life she chose to retreat to Essex when she was friendless and looking for peace, which could readily indicate an instinctive return to the shire of her birth.

Wherever she came from, and whatever her date of birth (never proven), she was certainly in the ageing queen's retinue by the end of 1366, and not in a menial role but as part of the queen's personal staff. This means that Alice had survived the Black Death that raged in East Anglia prior to her royal appointment, a period in history when half of England's population of around four million was wiped out. Because her mother and father are both shadowy figures in the chronicles, she could have been orphaned at an early age, like so many children at the time.

The queen, Philippa of Hainault, had married Edward III in 1327. Although the Hainault of her name indicates her roots in France, rather than any links to Hainault in Essex, she too had an Essex connection, her favourite retreat being a rural, unostentatious dwelling in the woods at Havering. Philippa, French born, was admired by everyone for her pious and courteous nature, and she was in her fifties and in declining health when Alice joined her at Havering. The queen liked to surround herself with youth and beauty, and it seems that Alice reminded her of her own young self.

It appears that Alice became the king's mistress in about 1364. This was the year when courtier Richard Lyons was commanded by Edward to allow Alice to go where she wished without restrictions. Nevertheless, Alice was among those welcome at the queen's bedside as her health deteriorated, sharing the vigil with the king. After Philippa's death in 1369 (possibly of the plague – records vary), Alice was among those to have received a bequest for her services. The king's order to the Exchequer to carry out Philippa's wishes referred to Alice as 'our beloved damsel' and their relationship now became public knowledge.

The king must have regarded Alice as a source of rejuvenation now that he was in his late fifties, and pre-occupied by the ongoing war with France and the tainted triumphs of his son, latterly known as the Black Prince. Her constant presence was certainly a source of comfort to Edward, and they shared an interest in acquiring money and the power that went with it.

Although Alice was clever enough to ensure that she stayed on good terms with the king's sons – Edward (the Black Prince) and John of Gaunt – she knew her situation was precarious. She therefore urged the king to make her a gift of land, his first gift being the manor of Wendover in Hampshire, followed by the Essex manors of Gaynes and Steeple St Lawrence. As the king weakened, Alice encouraged him to battle on, giving her the opportunity to become the power behind the throne.

As manors gifted by the king could be taken away on a whim, she began to negotiate for property in her own right, offering her royal influence in exchange for a bargain, and this seems to have worked. She acquired several houses in the City of London and another in the village of Hammersmith, and she also slowly took control of courtly extravagance. Alice was the one who made decisions regarding the running of the royal palaces, including Havering, which was one of at least seven. The king moved from one to another dependent on whether he wanted to hunt, be near to London, or see what was happening in Scotland. So his mistress, now an uncrowned queen, was kept busy with arrangements for transportation, cleaning, staffing and with organising feasts and tournaments as well as with public expenditure.

Site of Gaynes Park Lodge, East. (Author's Collection)

A minor victory for Alice was the king's order, four years after Philippa's death, that she should be granted all Philippa's 'jewels, goods and chattels', allowing her not only to flaunt her position at palace functions, but also providing her with some security for her financial dealings.

More significantly, in 1374, the king announced a tournament in her honour as a celebration at the end of Lent. Alice was paraded in front of the rich and influential from far and near as the Lady of the Sun, bedecked in a gold cloak and ermine-trimmed gown. Such a display of chivalrous veneration was bound to annoy the Church, given her role as fornicator, and the paganism of the temporary title. For seven days of celebration, of jousting, eating, drinking, and merry-making, Alice the concubine was queen in all but name. Already unpopular with the women at court, perhaps because of her low-born status, she became more and more disliked and was not able to hang on to her relationship with the princes. It was not long before allegations of sorcery began to circulate, and there was also an allegation that Alice had been involved in the murder of a sailor, but no reason or details have been recorded – it seems merely that Alice was on the receiving end of ill-founded propaganda, or is there really, truly, no smoke without just a little bit of fire?

Additionally, over the years, Alice has acquired a reputation as an adulteress but in fact there is no confirmed evidence that her relationship began with the king before he was widowed, nor is there any evidence that she married Sir William de Windsor, a long-term friend to whom she may have been 'betrothed'. She bore at least two, possibly three, children by either the king or by Windsor.

However, once the king's favourite son, Edward, had died, he made no further attempt to defend her influence. He was weary of war, tired of being surrounded by death and went along with proposals to destroy her influence, resulting in her banishment, forfeiting lands and possessions. She had to swear, while kissing a crucifix, that she would never return to the king's presence.

The exposure of sexual immorality at court tainted the probity of the court in general, leaving the way clear for charges to be levied against everyone involved in her activities. As a result, a lot of powerful figures – such as John of Gaunt – jockeyed for a stronger position in influencing the king and in determining his successor. Gaunt took his revenge on anyone daring to question his policies by nullifying parliamentary proposals. The king was happy to approve Gaunt's activities in return for the cancellation of Alice's expulsion.

She was now able to hasten to his side at Eltham, but, with the onset of winter, they moved to Havering. This was where Edward made his will. It appears that Alice was content with his gifts during life, avoiding controversy by being excluded from his bequests. Although Edward felt obliged to spend the following Christmas at Westminster, he and Alice returned soon after to a quiet existence at Havering-atte-Bower. The king's jubilee in February was marked by formal recognition of all agreed pardons, including that of Alice. Her property was officially hers by legal right, as were the dead queen's jewels. An itemised list drawn up revealed her ownership of twenty-two manors plus other land.

Apparently suffering from the effects of a stroke, Edward lingered on until after St George's Day in 1377. He spent his final weeks in the royal palace of Sheen, and his final hours with only Alice at his bedside. The disease that killed him was described, at the time, and perhaps predictably, as 'inordinate lust of the flesh'. A story persists that Alice, when Edward had slipped away, stole the rings from his fingers before leaving – but the truth will never be known. A pre-agreed sentimental gift perhaps? His last-known gesture to her was of a more practical nature, and reprised his first-ever gift: two tuns (nearly 2,000 litres) of Gascony wine.

When Edward was buried in Westminster Abbey in July, Alice was not admitted to the funeral. With a new king on the throne (the Black Prince's son, Richard), a campaign of retaliation against Alice began. In spite of parliamentary pre-occupation with French raiders in the south of England, the Keeper of the Wardrobe was instructed to present a long list of items in Alice's possession alleged to be the property of the Crown. The list included jewels, furniture, clothing, even small items such as ribbons. Any creditors who had claims against Alice were also invited to step forward so that 'justice should be done them'. On the one hand, Alice's possessions could be said to add to the depleted Treasury, while on the other it appears that vengeance was a stronger motive.

Alice was charged with disobeying parliamentary instructions, but she was able to prove that she had observed their orders until Gaunt had them cancelled. She was also charged with influencing the king to pardon Richard Lyons, who had been attacked (like her) by parliament. For this latter charge, the only witness she could find who was willing and able to stand up and attest to her innocence proved unconvincing in court.

On the surface, this 'trial' was a travesty of justice, with Gaunt acting as a hostile witness, and resulted in Alice's banishment, which meant she had to quit the realm after being stripped of all her possessions. This was, in fact, hardly practical, given the hostilities between England and Europe at the time, but parliament just wanted her away from their vicinity. The decision to strip Alice of her assets without any need to show proof of fraud in obtaining such assets was a much harder blow. She fled with her two children to her manor of Gaines in Upminster, one of just a few properties in the area which she had managed to salvage as legally hers.

The mysterious William de Windsor, an Essex landowner, often thought to have married Alice even before her relationship with Edward, reappears at this juncture, and the couple now seemed to live openly as man and wife. Was William merely ensuring that he would have rights to Alice's property? He was charged with harbouring a woman under sentence of banishment, but in the end Alice was authorised to remain in the realm so long as her 'husband' was willing to keep her by his side, and the threat of banishment remained as a suspended sentence. So was this in fact another clever move by Alice? Or was William actually a man to be trusted?

William put up a good argument in parliament that Alice had not been tried by the King's bench, had not been permitted to be present during all proceedings, had not been given enough time to prepare her case or her witnesses, and had been tried in her single name although a 'married woman', bearing in mind that a single woman at that time could not usually enjoy personal rights of possession. As a result, Alice was given a full pardon, and Windsor was given possession of those manors and estates that Alice had obtained legally, giving her greater security with money to support herself and her daughters in Upminster. As for William, he disappears again from the scene, accepting the office of Governor of Cherbourg.

Alice has even been accused of involvement in the Peasants' Revolt which flared up in Essex in 1381. It seems likely that Alice was living in Gaines Manor when the revolt broke out, but there are no records that her home was looted or that her family were harmed, as so many manors and landowners were in that part of Essex. Not that this makes her a conspirator.

William returned from Cherbourg to assist King Richard in clearing the insurgents from Essex and was appointed a baron for his efforts, but, exhausted by the campaign, he returned to his family estate in Westmorland (Cumbria) – and not to Alice. He died there in 1384, with no mention of Alice in his will. Because of the amount of debts William left behind him, his executor travelled to Upminster to try to sort out the complex nature of any Essex inheritance, but was given short shrift by Alice – not surprisingly.

She now had another fight to resist the attempts of William's creditors to claim what she regarded as rightfully hers. Alice did manage to become socially accepted at court again, thanks to Richard, whose mother – the anti-Alice Joan of Kent – had died. Her next move was to institute proceedings in the civil courts against John de Windsor, her

Upminster church. (Author's Collection)

Gaynes Bridge, c. 1921. (Courtesy of Tony Benton)

nephew by marriage, accusing him of illegally detaining property belonging to her and her daughter, worth in all around half a million pounds. She won her case and John was sent to Newgate Prison.

By now, Alice was in her fifties, dreaming of redress, and she retired permanently to her manor at Upminster to brood upon her situation. Richard's abdication and death in 1399 left her with few friends at court. Her daughters had married and left their Essex home. She could look back on a life ending very differently to the harsh childhood she had experienced: a life where she had been, at one point, the wealthiest common-born woman in the country.

She died in 1400, and, although leaving her land and houses to her daughters, she did not forget her roots. She left £400 to be distributed among the poor of Upminster, gifts for her servants, and additional money for repairs to the roads in and around the village, as most of the houses in the village were on her land. Alice asked that she be buried in Upminster church, and she left one of her best oxen to be sold to provide the money for her grave, grave ornaments, candles, and for the chaplain. The amount of money (around a thousand pounds in current terms) would have provided quite a special memorial but it has long since disappeared during periodic renovation and rebuilding. Its current location, if it has not been destroyed, is unknown.

It is probable that her younger daughter, who inherited the manor of Gaines (also known as Gaines or Gaynes Park, or Theydon Garnon – its eleventh-century name) did not enjoy the property for very long, given the disputes around its ownership, and the house itself disappears from records in the seventeenth century. The name Gaynes, however, lives on in street names in the area.

Essex Witches

From the Sixteenth to the Twentieth Centuries

The list of women who achieved infamy as a result of accusations of witchcraft – especially during Matthew Hopkins' notorious witch hunt of the seventeenth century – is too extensive to do justice to them all. Local record offices and libraries are full of books devoted to the Essex witch hunt, and museums, such as Colchester Castle Museum, devote a lot of space to presenting some of the grim history.

But witches were not a seventeenth-century phenomenon. A century earlier, Queen Elizabeth I passed a law forbidding the use of 'invocations and conjurations of evil'. The first resultant trial took place in Chelmsford in 1566, with three women from Hatfield Peverel featured: Agnes Waterhouse, her daughter Joan and her neighbour Elizabeth Francis (or Frauncis). Agnes was in her sixties, with the appearance associated – still – with the stereotype of a witch. She had plenty of enemies and seems to have boasted of her 'ability' to destroy animals belonging to neighbours who upset her, or to cause illness and even death, helped by her 'familiar' – Satan the cat. It is hardly surprising that she was found guilty and sentenced to death by hanging, the first local victim of the new law.

Luckily, eighteen-year-old Joan escaped punishment, and Elizabeth Francis, who seems to have admitted to abortion and murder, served one year in prison. But the latter ended up on the gallows in 1579 when she was brought to court for the same offence for the third time, aged fifty. She tried to save herself by naming other practising witches, to no avail. Between 1570 and 1609 fifty-three Essex witches were hanged (not all female), a quarter of those indicted.

The biggest English witchcraft case of this period took place in 1582, again in Chelmsford. This case involved thirteen women from St Osyth and the surrounding area, including Ursula/Ursley Kemp(e) who was hanged after being found guilty of three counts of murder by witchcraft. Ursula looked the part thanks

A traditional image of a witch. (Author's Collection)

to the curvature of her spine and her arthritic limbs. She had learned how to use herbs – and 'hogges dunge' – as remedies in order to help with her own aches and pains. However, by using this skill to help others, she inadvertently drew the attention of a local magistrate, charged with the task of seeking out witches.

Ursula was interrogated and body-searched at St Clere's Hall in St Osyth, and additional teats were allegedly found, which were then believed to be used to suckle 'familiars'. She 'confessed' in February and was held first in the local lock-up known as the Cage (there is a plaque at this location) and then in Colchester Castle. Evidence was gathered against her from neighbours and relatives. These included her illegitimate son, Thomas Rabbett, aged just eight, who spoke in court of how the family cats sucked blood from his mother 'in the night time', and also her brother, Lawrence Kemp. Her brother seems to have been instrumental in accusing Ursula of murdering his wife, who had died following a number of arguments with her sister-in-law and who had taken medicine administered by Ursula.

Elizabeth Bennett, a married neighbour named by Ursula during the unpleasantness of her cross-questioning and cross-examination, confessed to bewitching several local residents to death including her next door neighbours, the Byet(te)s. (Note that the magistrate, Brian Darcey, had almost certainly promised both women 'favour' if they confessed). She, too, had attracted attention in the village as a result of her lesbian relationship with Mrs Bonner. It is also possible that she was epileptic which would explain the fits which singled her out. Mr Bonner was among those who gave evidence against her, not surprisingly perhaps. He made reference not only to his wife's relationship with Mrs Bennett but to how a kiss from Elizabeth had caused his wife's 'upper lippe' to swell until it was 'very bigge'. Elizabeth, too, was imprisoned at Colchester Castle before being hanged.

There is a postscript to the Ursula Kemp/Elizabeth Bennett story. In 1921, the skeleton of at least one woman was found in a garden in St Osyth. The excavation of the area revealed that she had been pinned to the ground with iron spikes through the joints, an ancient practice said to stop a witch's spirit escaping. A curved spine could be identified as that of Ursula's and the skeleton made a little money for the house's owner as an exhibit until 1932, when the house mysteriously burned to the ground. The grave was filled in but the bones were finally salvaged and removed to the Witchcraft Museum in Boscastle, Cornwall, in 1964. Slight traces of tar could still be seen on the shoulder blades, suggesting that she was dipped in tar before being hanged, probably just one of several forms of torture that she and Elizabeth endured.

St Osyth featured again in the witch hunts that took place east of Colchester at the time of the Civil War. King James was a firm believer in witches, and wanted to stamp out their influence even more than Elizabeth had; he even wrote several books on the subject. In 1645 alone, there were thirty-six witch trials in Essex. The self-styled Witchfinder General, Matthew Hopkins, had an associate in Mary Phillips, a midwife from Manningtree. This lady took on the task of searching the accused women for evidence in the form of teats or other identifying marks of the devil – warts, moles, even grazes. Her name appears as a witness on many of the assize records of Chelmsford witch trials during this period. He carried out his interrogations mainly at inns in Manningtree and Mistley but some seem to have taken place at Colchester Castle. His record was nineteen witches hanged in one day. As an incentive, Hopkins

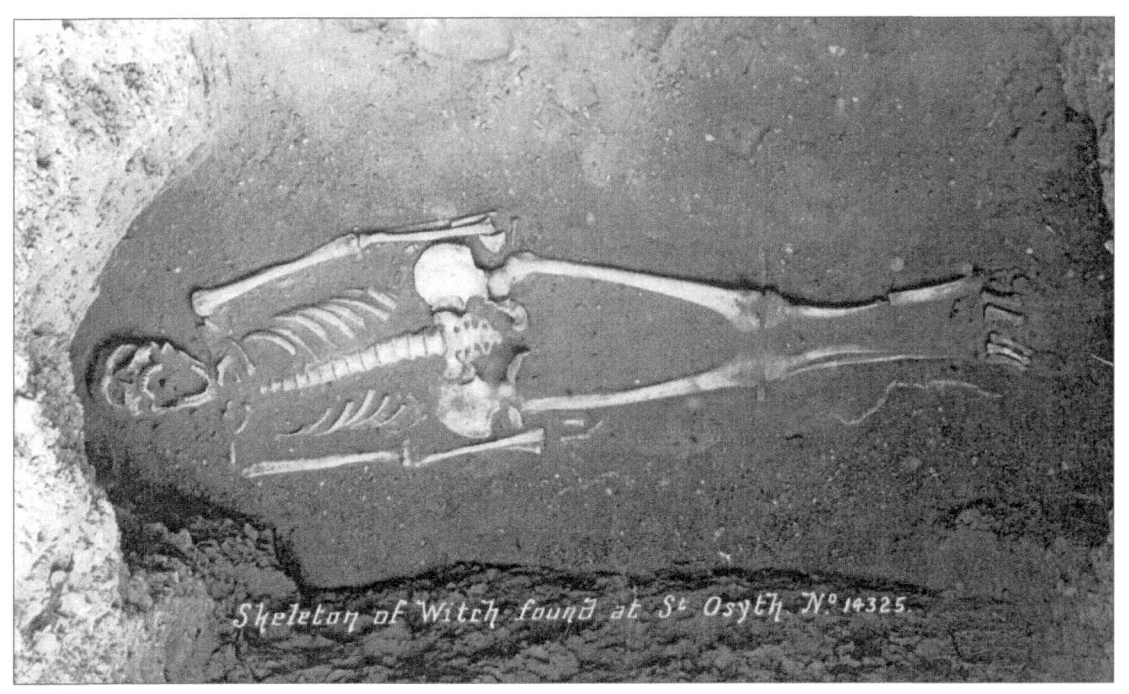

Skeleton of the St Osyth witch. (Courtesy of Phyll Hendy)

The plaque commemorating St Osyth 'cage'. (Courtesy of Cliff Hull)

Sarah Moore (pub sign).
(Courtesy of Mark Kimber)

was able to charge the local parish 20*s* for every witch found and it is thought that by the end of 1646 he had made the equivalent of £66,000.

Between 1560 and 1680 in Essex alone, 317 women were tried for witchcraft, and over 100 were hanged. Each victim of such injustice during the sixteenth and seventeenth centuries deserves to be foregrounded here, but let these few stories stand as examples for the many others.

Postscript: In 1736 George II repealed the laws which provided for alleged witches to be hanged on such flimsy evidence, but the accusations continue. There are many later accounts of witchcraft, including the nineteenth-century Sarah Moore of Leigh-on-Sea who was said to be able to put a spell on newborn babies so that they were born with a facial deformity, and to 'set fire' to children who upset her. Even as recently as the early 1900s a 'witch' by the name of Hart was documented as living in Latchingdon with her familiars – a vast army of imps, small animals with 'fiery red eyes'.

Elizabeth Blount

c. 1500–c. 1540

Elizabeth is not an Essex girl at all, but her connection with Essex could have changed the history of the British monarchy – so she cannot be ignored. 'Bessie' seems to have been brought up in a comfortable household in Shropshire as the second daughter (of eight surviving children) of Sir John Blount and his wife, Katherine. The family served the county rather than the court, i.e. as sheriffs or justices of the peace. As for Bessie, she became a maid of honour to Katherine of Aragon in 1512, the ideal job to find a suitable husband. Her duties involved accompanying the queen to devotions and at mealtimes, sewing, studying Latin, French, riding, singing, music and dancing. In return, she was paid around 100s a year.

As a well-educated, musical and literary member of the court, and as someone reputedly more beautiful than Anne Boleyn, her contemporary, she could not fail to attract the attention of King Henry VIII. He seems to have initially paid her attention at the New Year revels of 1514 when

Elizabeth Blount. (Author's Collection)

The Priory, Blackmore. (Author's Collection)

Katherine was recovering from the loss of her new baby. He was no doubt able to spend more time with young Bessie once Katherine was pregnant for the seventh time, in 1518. In fact, their affair was longer lasting than many of Henry's, except perhaps Mary Boleyn. No other suitors are recorded for Bessie at the time.

The result of this relationship was the birth of Henry Fitzroy in 1519, born in about June. It was not unusual for court mistresses to give birth to their illegitimate offspring in religious houses, and Bessie was sent to the twelfth-century St Laurence's Priory at Blackmore, near Brentwood, to give birth. The priory was not particularly large or significant, but it was only twenty-five miles from London. Cardinal Wolsey made all the arrangements, a man who had also provided for his own mistresses and children. Bessie was not quartered with the holy men, but allowed the use of a nearby house – Jericho – which served as the prior's main residence.

By choosing a priory rather than a nunnery, Wolsey was perhaps reducing the chances of gossip. After all, Henry would not have wanted to advertise another failed pregnancy if Elizabeth had been unlucky. It also meant that the king could visit more openly. After all, his wife had a favourite residence close by, Pyrgo Palace at Havering-atte-Bower. The confinement and birth were certainly kept under wraps, with no references in diplomatic correspondence of the period. If Wolsey was indeed the boy's godfather, however, as some have alleged, that would have spoken volumes.

It seems that the king visited Bessie and their son often enough at Blackmore to prompt a standing joke at court that he had 'gone to Jericho'. Henry was the king's first 'recognised' son and 'Bless 'ee, Bessie Blount' became a popular saying at the time. She had, after all, provided evidence that Henry could produce sons: 'Fitzroy' means sired by a regent. (There was another possible illegitimate son as a result of another of Henry's many affairs – with Elizabeth Bryan, a very young friend of Bessie's.)

Assuming that Bessie's blessing was reported to Katherine, it is not that surprising that the queen went into premature labour and lost her own newborn son. By September Cardinal Wolsey had arranged for Bessie to be married to Lord Gilbert Tailboys, a ward of the crown, and a match which Henry may well have regarded as a reward for Bessie's 'services'. She was also assured of £200 per year for life from property granted to her by Henry, and continued to enjoy his favour throughout her life with Gilbert. The couple settled in Lincolnshire and had three children of their own.

In the meantime, young Henry, looking so much like his father, had become the king's pride and joy. He was brought up with the Tailboys' other children but was created Earl of Nottingham at the age of six. This was the first illegitimate son raised to the peerage since the twelfth century. By the age of eight, he was Duke of Richmond, Admiral of England, Ireland and Normandy. Such recognition of the boy amounted to recognition of his status as the king's son, and, had he lived, he could have made a play for the English throne given the lack of male 'issue'.

Young Henry's only ongoing connection with Essex were his visits to the hunting grounds around the River Lea. His death at St James's Palace from an unidentified and sudden chest infection came just as an act was going through parliament to enable the king to nominate him as heir. He was only seventeen when he died, shortly after becoming betrothed. Fiction writers could make his end, given its timing, far more interesting.

Above: St Laurence Priory Church. (Author's Collection)

Left: Blackmore village sign. (Author's Collection)

When Gilbert died in 1530, the opportunity of legitimising the boy by the king's marriage to Bessie was passed over for the very different opportunity offered to the king by Anne Boleyn.

The royal connection lives on in Blackmore, with the gold crown which features on the village sign on the green. The priory was, of course, affected by the 1525 dissolution, but the priory church remains, formerly the priory chapel. There are several other local reminders of Elizabeth Blount and her Essex connection – apart from the now-undistinguished remains (of Jericho House?) next to the church, there is also Little Jericho House and Jericho Cottage nearby. Incidentally, the village stream which fed the moat surrounding the priory buildings, and which led to the nearby River Can, was once known as 'the Jordan'.

Elizabeth doesn't seem to figure in Essex again, as, after Lord Gilbert's death, she remarried – Lord Clinton of Lincoln. This union produced another three daughters, and Bessie was to die of consumption, perhaps following in the footsteps of the king's son. A king's son born in Essex, don't forget.

Mary Boleyn

c. 1499–1543

The elder daughter of Thomas Boleyn was not born in Essex, but perhaps in Norfolk or Kent, her father being a substantial landowner. Rochford Hall was owned by her grandfather until her father inherited it in 1515. It seems likely she spent some of her early childhood there, however, visiting her grandparents. She certainly spent her later years there. There was also a palace at Hunsdon House, near Harlow, known in Tudor times as the 'nursery palace' where Mary and her younger siblings, Elizabeth and Edward, would have spent time together.

Earliest records are of her being despatched to Paris as maid of honour to Princess Mary Tudor in 1514, when Mary married King Louis XII. The Boleyn girl stayed on in the court of Queen Claude when Mary returned to England after Louis' death, and it was there that she began to acquire a reputation as a young woman of 'easy virtue'. She is even reputed to have had an affair with the heir to the French throne – later to become King Francis I – who is recorded as describing her as a 'great whore, the most infamous of all' and as his 'English mare'.

Her father brought her back to the court of Queen Catherine in 1519 and made sure that she soon married – William Carey, a gentleman of the privy chamber. Henry VIII was the chief guest at their wedding at Greenwich Palace, and Will, a descendant of John of Gaunt, was a royal companion in the tiltyard and the tennis court. Mary joined the list of Henry's mistresses just a few years later (some say earlier); certainly by 1523 she had become enough of a fixture for Henry to name a ship after her. William Carey was granted several gifts of land by Henry, and this has been seen as a reward for overlooking his wife's adultery. Mary's father was probably similarly recompensed for turning a blind eye.

Her relationship with the king was unusual in that Mary was married, but

Mary Boleyn. (Author's Collection)

Rochford Hall remains, 2007.
(Author's Collection)

it did mean that Henry could deny paternity of any children. Young Henry was born in 1526 but the boy was just as likely to have been William's, as there were signs that Henry's affair with Mary was over by then. There are historians who have produced 'evidence' of Henry's paternity, but such evidence is generally circumstantial. What historians do agree on is that Mary was more attractive than Anne, although she seems to have been less ambitious and far less manipulative.

When William died in 1528 (of a 'sweating sickness'), Henry ordered Thomas Boleyn to take Mary under his roof and maintain her, granting her an annuity of £100. However, in 1534 she secretly married William Stafford, a commoner. The relationship was regarded as a misalliance because of his lack of status and his family connection to the unpopular Duke of Buckingham. She was no longer received at court – thanks to her sister – and settled for a life of obscurity at Rochford Hall, the Boleyn's family home in Essex, with Stafford and her two children from the marriage to Carey. The Staffords had at least one child, a son who died at a young age.

Anecdotal local sources reveal that William Stafford was known to remove bells from local churches (including three from Rochford) which he sold to repair sea walls. More seriously, Anne's execution in 1536 was followed by the death of Thomas Boleyn and his wife, and Mary inherited some of the Boleyn properties in Essex. Her son inherited Rochford Hall when she died in 1543, and Henry VIII made further provision for her – or their – children. Her daughter, Catherine, was appointed maid of honour to Anne of Cleves and young Henry became a member of the royal household.

Mary has come to belated fame as a result of recent fictionalised accounts of her life, but she will always remain in the shadow of the notorious Anne, who seems to have been the less promiscuous of the two sisters.

Anne Boleyn

c. 1500–36

Anne, like her sister, was probably born in Thomas Boleyn's Norfolk property (Blickling Hall) rather than in Essex. But she certainly spent time with her grandparents at Rochford Hall before being despatched to France to the court of Louis and Mary. She was probably not attractive enough to acquire a flighty reputation – very dark eyes and hair, skin that bordered on sallow, unfashionably small-breasted. Whether she had an extra finger (also a sign of witchcraft) is difficult to substantiate, although if she did indeed start a fashion for long sleeves covering the hands then that would seem a good enough reason.

Returning to England in 1521, Anne was appointed maid of honour to Queen Catherine from Rochford Hall. Regardless of her appearance, it seems that her personality, her wit and her courtly accomplishments all combined to attract the king, among others. Anne, however, refused the king's advances, making her all the more attractive in his eyes, a man not used to rejection. It seems unlikely that Anne's refusal was out of virtue, even though many historians have sprung to defend her from subsequent accusations of manoeuvring her way to the throne.

Henry's pursuit of Anne may well have extended beyond her court appearances. He was fond of hunting in the forests around Rochford and could well have met up with Anne if she had visited Rochford Hall, which seems likely. Another local venue for their courtship was at New Hall, Boreham, near Chelmsford. This mansion was referred to as Beaulieu by Henry VIII, who had bought it from Anne's father, Thomas, in 1516 for £1,000 and subsequently spent no less than £17,000 on it! By 1527, the couple were planning to marry, and there is some evidence to account for Anne visiting Beaulieu that year as one of the queen's ladies-in-waiting, giving them the opportunity to hatch a marriage plan with some of Henry's most trusted advisors and friends.

Anne Boleyn (pub sign). (Courtesy of Mark Kimber)

If it had not been for Anne's stubborn refusal to become the king's mistress, the whole course of English history – and of Christendom – could have been very different. Even expensive gifts such as gold fabric worth £74 – a fortune in the sixteenth century – did not persuade her otherwise. As it was, the only way for Henry to get into Anne's bed was by marrying her, breaking with Rome and divorcing Catherine. They did jump the gun, however, because it seems that Anne was pregnant at the time of their secret marriage in 1533, secret because Henry's marriage had not yet been nullified. Part of Anne's dowry upon marriage were cottages on Strand Wharf, Leigh (now Leigh-on-Sea).

During the fairly limited honeymoon period that this famous couple enjoyed, Henry is said to have built a tower atop his favourite hunting lodge, Boleyn Castle at West Ham, an area then considered part of Essex. The purpose of the tower was for Anne to be able to see the shipping on the river – but it was also used, legend has it, to 'imprison' Anne if Henry's jealousy was aroused. Further evidence of Henry's attachment was his gift to Anne of Roydon Hall Manor at Epping Forest, a property he had acquired in 1531.

Unfortunately for Anne, of course, she failed to produce the heir Henry needed – and how galling it must have been that both Elizabeth Blount and Anne's sister, Mary, had produced healthy boys. It is interesting that subsequent theories about Anne's witch-like abilities have suggested that she did indeed try to poison young Richmond

Tower of London execution block.
(Author's Collection)

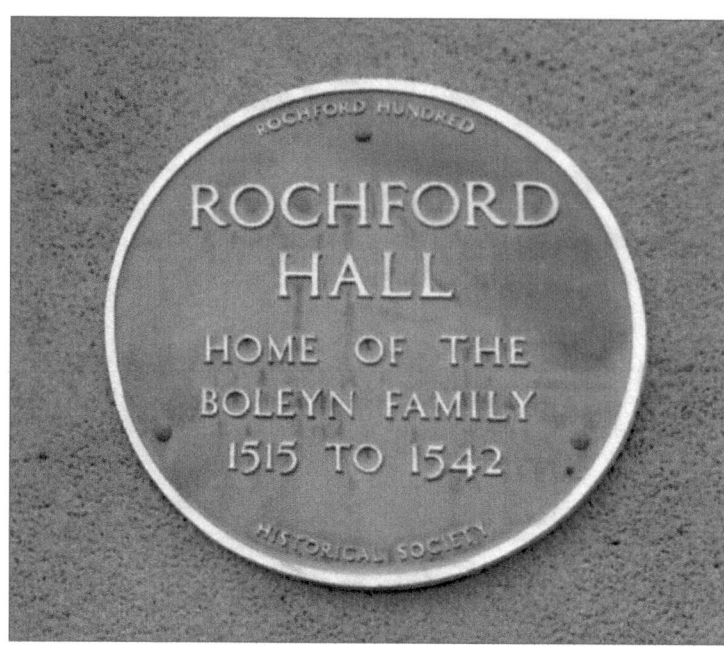

Plaque at Rochford Hall, 2007. (Author's Collection)

(Elizabeth Blount's son). Henry did give a magnificent ball at Beaulieu upon the birth of Princess Elizabeth in 1533, but no girl, no matter how feisty, could make up for the lack of sons.

So that Henry could marry yet again, Anne was accused of treason, adultery, even incest, the guilty verdict resulting – not unexpectedly – in the death sentence. Death by the axe was a terrifying prospect and a swordsman was called from France to the Tower of London to sever the reputedly narrow neck with a sword instead of the usual axe. There is a local legend which suggests that her severed head was smuggled to East Horndon and buried under the altar tomb of All Saints' church.

Finally, it is said to be Anne's – rather than the more appropriate Mary's – ghost that haunts Rochford Hall, the links with Essex continuing in death as in life. Having said that, she is also reputed to haunt the area of Boleyn Castle and the grounds of New Hall.

Mary I (Bloody Mary)

1516–58

The infamous reputation of this royal daughter of Henry VIII and Catherine of Aragon was far more bloodthirsty than that accorded to the mistresses in previous chapters. Following the short reign of Edward VI, and Lady Jane Grey's even briefer attempt to take her place, Mary's reign (from 1553) tried returning the country to Catholicism. Part of her grand plan – after Jane's execution – was to marry Philip of Spain, put down those who revolted against her, and persecute Protestants. It is this latter trait that earned her the name of Bloody Mary.

The childhood of Princess Mary, however, was less violent. She spent part of her early years at Wanstead House, returning as a guest of Lord Rich before her accession and coronation. This was an extensive estate partly in Epping and partly in Waltham. Ingatestone Hall and South Weald Hall in Brentwood both have Marian connections.

Mary is also believed to have spent time with her younger siblings at Havering Palace on the hill above Romford. During one visit at least, ambassadors from Portugal came to inspect Mary at Havering Palace – as a possible bride for one of their princes. Mary, however, was a tiny, thin young woman, and although she was musical and intelligent, these inspections did not have a favourable outcome.

Another home for the princess for a number of years was at New Hall, Boreham, near Chelmsford, known as Beaulieu. She is known to have lived here from 1532,

New Hall, near Chelmsford. (Author's Collection)

Copped Hall, Epping. (Author's Collection)

when she had been forced to separate from her mother, whose marriage had been found to be conveniently illegal. By 1534, Mary's large household was reduced substantially to a size appropriate for a 'royal bastard' and she herself was reduced in status from princess to lady. She wrote to the king from New Hall asserting her rightful claim to the throne.

It was not until 1544, however, that King Henry re-established her as heir apparent to Edward, and Edward granted New Hall to Mary for life on his accession. Her adherence to Catholicism was a problem for Edward and his advisors once he was on the throne (from 1547). At this time it seems that he allowed his Catholic sister to live at Copped (or Copt) Hall in Epping. There she remained, effectively, a prisoner, but with no qualms about celebrating Catholic Mass. The king showed his displeasure at her behaviour in ignoring the royal command by sending a series of influential messengers, but these she dismissed with scorn. She told them she would readily die for her faith and would fend for herself if necessary, having 'learned how many loaves of bread be made of a bushel of wheat'.

Not long afterwards, it seems that Mary moved back to New Hall. It was not unusual for the royal family to move around, of course, leaving a grubby palace behind them to be cleaned while they stayed at one that had been prepared for them. She is still recorded as being under house arrest, but her situation worsened when the royal chamberlain visited her there to inform her that she was to be stripped of her title of princess. Again, her response was rebellious. She declared that she had no doubt that she was 'the King's true daughter, born in good and lawful matrimony'.

By 1549, she is recorded as living at the manor house at Woodham Walter. She had apparently announced that plague had broken out in New Hall, allowing her and a few of her household to move on without suspicion. Records exist detailing gifts from leading townsmen of capons, wild fowl, a turkey cock and hen, 'in reward to my lady Mary's Grace at her last being at Woodham'. The location meant a boat could be constantly kept ready should she need to escape to the continent if danger threatened. The manor was among pleasant woods, hills and sheltered valleys, two miles from the Blackwater. It was actually owned by Henry Fitzwalter, a Catholic supporter.

The Duke of Northumberland, Edward's Protector, was a worry for Mary's followers who felt that her life was in danger. Fitzwalter sheltered Mary while she made plans in 1550 to escape to Holland – a Catholic country – in a ship sent by her uncle, Emperor Charles. After initial discussions with his ambassador, Van der Delft, who could not dissuade Mary from escape, the first plan was for Mary and her ladies to board his boat at the Hythe. However, a peasant uprising had meant an increase in the watch, and such a departure would be challenged.

The next plan was that the emperor's warships would ride at anchor in the Blackwater Estuary, ostensibly to attack pirates, and from there an innocent-looking corn boat, commanded by Delft's agent (Jehan Dubois) would make contact with her via the port at Maldon. Dubois made contact with Sir Robert Rochester, the controller of Mary's household, but Sir Robert was concerned about Mary losing her hope of succession if King Edward (a sickly individual) died when she was abroad.

Mary I. (Author's Collection)

Nevertheless, Dubois met with Mary who told him she needed a couple of days to prepare. It seems she was concerned at compromising her own position. As for Dubois, he was concerned at the large amount of luggage – clothes and jewels – that Mary wanted to take with her. He tried to reassure her that everything she needed was waiting for her in Holland. She eventually agreed to be ready in the early hours when the tide was right, but Rochester intervened, telling Mary that warships had been spotted and suspicions aroused, resulting in the arrest of the corn boat.

This news shattered Mary's nerve, although it seems that Rochester made up the story to panic Mary into refusing to flee. Dubois was actually able to leave in the 'corn boat' – albeit in a hurry, apparently leaving an important crew member behind – with no attempts at restraint.

Hostility to Protestantism and to the new prayer book was not a good idea, following on the heels of insurgency in Norfolk and Cornwall. Although Mary declared that she would 'rather suffer death than stain (her) conscience', she returned to New Hall. Back 'home' a military presence had been intensified, and her chaplain had been forced to flee to the Catholic stronghold of Yorkshire after being threatened with arrest for celebrating Mass.

Pressure was put on Mary to return to court, far from the sea, but visits from Chancellor Richard Rich of Great Leighs Priory and Sir William Petre of Ingatestone could not persuade her to leave New Hall. Mary pleaded ill health, and Rich suggested that a change of air would do her good, but she did not budge until March 1551 when she was ordered to Edward's presence, where he berated her for hearing Mass. She was allowed to return to New Hall as long as her Masses were not open to outsiders, but this concession was short-lived. Edward soon declared that even a private mass would not be allowed, and Mary's staff were put into the Tower for a year, and her chaplains traced and arrested.

When King Edward died of consumption in 1553 and the princess was able to proclaim herself queen, the people of Maldon supported her claim against that of Lady Jane Grey. She was crowned queen in 1553, during which year she leased New Hall to Sir Thomas Warton, a member of her Privy Council. In his case, he could celebrate mass freely with his family in the house where his former mistress had been harassed. At thirty-eight, the new queen was a delicate, domestic, rather unhappy individual, dedicated to her faith. She became the first English woman to be crowned without a civil war breaking out.

Entrance to Ingatestone Hall, 2007. (Author's Collection)

It was only after her marriage to Philip II of Spain in 1554 that her religious fanaticism and murderous nature surfaced. The marriage was arguably the most unpopular royal marriage in English history, Spain being no friend to England. But she ignored her father-in-law's advice to tread gently in her religious reform and her religious zeal created 273 Protestant Marian martyrs. With the help of the equally fanatical Bishop of London, Edward Bonner, many Protestant bishops were deposed. Cranmer and Latimer were burned at the stake. Protestants faced fire or exile as Mass returned to the churches. She also damaged her reputation with non-religious members of the public by excluding Princess Elizabeth from the succession and forcing her into near-solitary confinement.

Essex suffered acutely from her fanatical and brutal tenacity, with ten Colchester men executed in the flames under the castle walls in 1557. Nine further Colchester men and a woman also suffered the same fate during Mary's reign. Scores of dissenters from Essex were tied together and dragged along the streets of London on a single rope. A memorial at Stratford recalls 1556 when eleven men and two women were tied together in a holocaust witnessed by a vast multitude. More than seventy Essex people died including a 'cripple' from Barking, a Hadleigh doctor, a Brentwood youth, a Horndon farmer, a Chigwell rector, and others from Braintree, Manningtree, Rochford and Saffron Walden. There are a number of monuments to these martyrs spread around the county, including those at Rochford and Rayleigh, victims of the religious intolerance which still lingers in parts of the world.

Mary's reign was thankfully limited to five years. She produced no children, although some sources reveal that she thought she was pregnant shortly before her death, while others attribute the 'symptoms' to stomach cancer. There was dancing in the street at the news of her death in 1558, and Elizabeth, then imprisoned in the Tower, was to be released and given the news that she was the new Queen of England.

Katherine Seymour (née Grey)

c. 1540–68

Mary Tudor's granddaughter seems to have been far less dour and downright nasty than her ancestor. Her fame is not as widespread as her sister, Jane, who lived such a short, sweet, sad life, was queen so briefly and died so violently. Katherine's links with Essex were more extensive than Jane's, and she is included under the description of 'infamous' because she made some serious errors of judgment which sullied her reputation.

Katherine and Jane lived out their childhood in Leicestershire, moving to London as part of their father's (Henry Grey, Duke of Suffolk) plan to put Jane onto the throne. In 1553 the scheming Henry arranged for Jane to marry Lord Guildford Dudley (the Duke of Northumberland's son) and for his younger daughter to marry Henry Herbert (the Earl of Pembroke's son). However, it seems Katherine's marriage was not consummated and it was dissolved after Mary came to the throne.

By 1559, Katherine's father and sister had been executed for treason, and her mother had died. Now that Elizabeth was on the throne, her ex-father-in-law was keen on re-establishing his son's marriage to Katherine who had a claim to the throne as granddaughter of Mary Tudor. But Katherine had been in love with the dashing young Edward Seymour, Earl of Hertford, for a number of years by this time. Hertford was similarly attracted to the docile Katherine, by all accounts pretty and adoring. Regardless of their mutual attraction, no one of royal blood could marry unless the queen had given her authorisation. If they went ahead, then it was regarded as treason. Katherine's mother had made several unsuccessful attempts to use her influence with the queen to obtain royal approval for the young couple's union.

In spite of this, Katherine and Hertford decided to risk a secret marriage at his home,

Katherine Grey. (Author's Collection)

aided and abetted by his sister. It seems remarkable, with hindsight, that Katherine did not take warning from what had happened to her sister and father. It was also considered disgusting at the time for a well-born female to put emotion before custom and duty. Regardless of the 'immoral' and 'unlawful' nature of what she had done, the marriage was hastily consummated and, within six months, Katherine was pregnant.

When she discovered she was expecting, Hertford was in France, so she turned to Lord Robert Dudley for advice. He promptly informed the queen, resulting in Katherine's imprisonment in the Tower and a demand for Hertford's return from Paris.

Young Edward was born in the Tower in May 1561 and declared illegitimate following a commission to judge the status of the marriage – the minister had disappeared, leaving no evidence of the ceremony's legality. This suited Elizabeth because it discredited Katherine and invalidated any claim she may have had to the throne. The couple were, however, allowed unofficial conjugal visits while continuing their confinement in the Tower, and Katherine gave birth to a second son, Thomas, in 1563. Such inappropriate behaviour meant that a fine of £15,000 was imposed – an enormous amount of money at the time. From here on, they were only allowed to exchange letters and she never saw her husband again.

Lord Grey wrote to the queen's secretary regarding Katherine's 'woefull life' and pleaded for renewed royal favour on her behalf. As a result, Katherine was taken under strict house arrest to the home of her uncle at Pyrgo (or Pirgo) Palace in Havering parish when Thomas was just six months old. Elizabeth's decision to move Katherine and her sons to Essex may well have had something to do with the threat of plague in London. The palace, purchased by Henry VIII as a second residence and an alternative to the ageing Havering Palace, was given to Katherine's uncle by Elizabeth. From Pyrgo, Katherine frequently petitioned Dudley to secure a pardon from the queen, but was not to be forgiven so readily. The queen had even heard earlier stories of a plot by Philip II of Spain – her sworn enemy – to marry Katherine off to his son.

Lord John Grey, her uncle, died at the end of 1564, and Katherine, still in custody, was transferred to the control of Sir William Petre of Ingatestone Hall. When Sir William declared that he could no longer afford to keep her, in spite of financial assistance being provided by Hertford, Sir John Wentworth of Halstead took on the role for a while. Katherine was finally moved out of Essex at the end of 1567 (when Sir John died) to Cockfield Hall in Suffolk. Her lengthy spell in custody reflected the protracted arguments going on in parliament about her own claim to the succession. In this regard, she was assisted by John Hales MP to establish the legality of her marriage. Such support infuriated the queen and Hales, too, ended up in the Tower. Elizabeth, in the meantime, categorically refused to name her successor in the absence of any children of her own, but she was certainly unsympathetic to Katherine's claim. If Katherine broke the accepted, unwritten rules regarding the marriage of princesses, then she deserved to be punished.

Among Lord Grey's letters to the Queen pleading Katherine's cause, there are references to her state of mind as verging on suicidal. One letter claims that Katherine 'wolde to God' she was buried, but for her 'lorde' and 'childrerne'. He also indicated that she was not eating and it could well be that Katherine developed an eating disorder – possibly anorexia – during her years of imprisonment. This may well have prompted her early death at the age of just twenty-eight.

Ingatestone Hall. (Author's Collection)

Eventually, nearly forty years after her death, her marriage was finally declared legal, leaving her sons as heirs to the throne. Memories of her indiscretion, disobedience, obstinacy and disgrace live on in spite of her short, rather sad life.

Elizabeth I

1533–1603

Another queen! This one was nearly as infamous for persecuting Catholics as her half-sister was for persecuting Protestants. Essex has a lot of royal links, and Elizabeth in particular seems to have been fond of the county as well as of the person: Robert Devereux, Earl of Essex, one of her favourites.

On Mary's death in 1558, Elizabeth walked from the Tower of London as the new queen. It would be insulting to the reader to give an account of the life of this famous royal, a life so often documented and filmed. Suffice it to say we are talking of a great leader engaged in a lifelong struggle to establish England as a free country with a reputation as one of the strongest nations in the civilised world. The fact that she showed some cruelty along the way, with a level of indifference to suffering and even some petty malice is, to some extent, understandable, if debatable. She was surrounded by treachery and plots which could have been curtailed if she had married or produced a named heir, neither of which she apparently felt obliged to do.

Under Elizabeth, two hundred Catholics were martyred as traitors, though only one in Essex (John Paine, a priest who was hanged, drawn and quartered at Chelmsford in 1582). In spite of this, she was generally popular among the general public who returned her affection and supported her ambition. She had the Marian bishops removed, although, to be fair, they were treated quite leniently.

Where Essex was concerned, she actually disposed of many royal properties in the area – including New Hall/Beaulieu – as gifts or rewards, having inherited in excess of sixty properties from her father, Henry VIII. It seems that Elizabeth, understandably, never spent money on houses she did not intend to occupy. Copped Hall, for instance, was granted to Sir Thomas Heneage, thus avoiding some heavy maintenance expenses. Similarly, Pyrgo Palace near Havering (also known as Portgore – Park Gate) was given to Lord John Grey, the uncle of Lady Jane Grey.

What is of additional Essex interest are her 'progresses' through the county, visiting one royal palace after another, or staying with the cream of the upper strata of society who were honoured – although nearly bankrupted – by her presence. The accounts of property owners such as Sir William Petre of Ingatestone Hall detail the outlay for fish, game, fruit, as well as necessary foodstuffs (e.g. bread and beer), and the costs of the staff of cooks, brewers, bakers, bricklayers, carpenters and labourers, not to mention the necessity for providing Elizabeth herself with an expensive gift such as an ornate piece of jewellery. Prior to the arrival of the royal party – as many as five hundred of them – the luggage party would arrive, with its innumerable carts, including a portable bath, and then the heralds and the trumpeters would precede the queen herself. Some

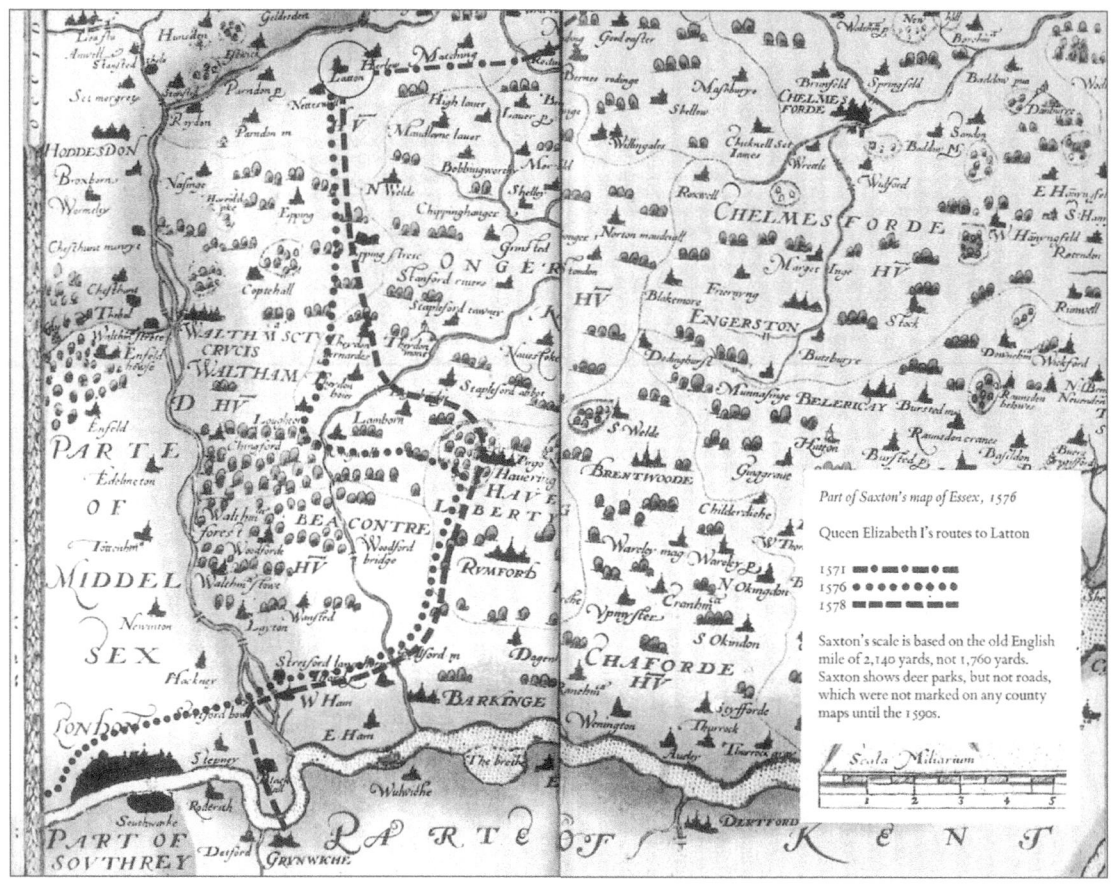

Elizabeth's progresses through Essex. (Harlow Development Corporation)

of the family would have to move out to make space for the queen's party, utilising accommodation in local inns or even tents if necessity demanded. Church bells would ring and crowds would flock to see her.

The queen would certainly have known Essex better than most areas because at least seven of her progresses started out at the palace of Havering-atte-Bower, high above Romford, with spectacular views. Such progresses were slow, on poor roads, in forested, empty countryside; and it was rare for Elizabeth to stay for more than two days at any one location. There are details of the 1561 progress through Essex, for instance, with the queen visiting Loughton Hall (one of her own royal manors), Ingatestone Hall, New Hall, Felix Hall near Kelvedon, Colchester (possibly St John's Abbey), and St Osyth Priory, before moving on to Suffolk by water. Her return was via Hedingham Castle, Gosfield Hall, Leez (Priory) and Hallingbury Morley, now Great Hallingbury. Such brief visits were not merely social, however, because there are many accounts of councils held during her visits. At least two of her 'hosts' – Thomas Lucas of St John's Abbey and John Cutts of Horeham Hall – were subsequently knighted.

Essex was the location chosen for another progress in 1568 – to Havering, Copped Hall, and Giddy Hall near Romford (hence the contemporary name of Gidea). In 1571 there was Audley End, Hor(e)ham Hall ('Thackstead'), Mark Hall at 'Latton' and Leez again. Other progresses added further venues: Ongar Castle, Feering Bury, Gosfield Hall, Smallbridge Hall (near Bures St Mary), Harwich, Layer Marney, Maldon and Moulsham Hall (near Chelmsford). There was another visit to Essex in 1576 and another, perhaps in 1578, which was longer than usual, perhaps to escape plague raging in London. Stopovers included Havering, Latton, Audley, Moyns (Steeple Bumpstead?), Horeham Hall, plus Rayne Hall near Braintree, Rookwood Hall at Abbess 'Roothing', Gaynes Park at 'Theydon Garnon', Loughton Hall, Wanstead – the home of the Earl of Leicester – and Stanstead Abbots.

Elizabeth I. (Author's Collection)

The houses she did not visit were either too far out of the way or owned by those unacceptable in court circles, often for religious reasons. Queen Elizabeth hated the smell of woad and would not have a woad mill within five miles of any of her palaces. At Stanstead, a woad manufacturing centre, visitors were 'constrained to stop their noses as . . . the stink is so grate'. The longest and most frequent visits were to New Hall and Havering.

Apart from having a hand in the deaths of so many Catholics, it was Elizabeth, of course, who was responsible for the command to execute Mary Queen of Scots in 1587, following the latter's involvement in plots to overthrow her. The other bloody period of her reign was prompted, in part, by her rejection of Philip II of Spain. Obviously, her role in the thousands of Spanish deaths as a result of the Spanish Armada was distanced by her position as queen, a woman frustratingly unable to go into battle.

Tilbury achieved fame in 1588 when over five thousand soldiers encamped at Tilbury Fort were confronted with their queen astride a white horse urging them to continue their effective defence against the Spanish Armada: 'I am come . . . in the midst and heat of the battle, to live or die amongst you all.' In her silver breast plate with red wig and huge pearls she made a striking leader, and her reference to her 'weak and feeble body' with the 'heart and stomach of a king' struck just the right note among the men standing in awe before her, men who were aware of the mighty Spanish force with as many as 50,000 men approaching by sea. The night before she had stayed at Arderne Hall at Horndon with a relative of Lord Rich, captain of a 'company of lances'. How the 1,000 horses and 2,000 'foot' escorting her were housed is quite remarkable.

After her famous speech, she would have planned on returning to London by water in her state barge, but she was overtaken by a violent storm. This meant landing at Purfleet (seven miles up river from Tilbury) and probably spending the night two miles inland at Belhus Park in Aveley – legends abound around her visit to this house, although no real evidence of such a visit has been forthcoming. Her huge entourage would again have need of accommodation.

Even into her fifties, the queen was said to have enjoyed hunting, favouring Epping Forest with its hunting lodge on the edge of Chingford Plain. The lodge was originally

Tilbury Fort. (Author's Collection)

Elizabeth I's signature. (Author's Collection)

built for her father in 1543 but was one of the places she was willing to take on after his death. Sir William Addison, an iconic Essex writer, speculates that the building was more of a shooting gallery, with courtiers firing on 'beasts of chase' that had been driven in their direction. It could equally have started life as a spectator-stand.

When Elizabeth died at the age of seventy, she had been a successful ruler for forty-four years in spite of her ruthless streak. However, her success at strengthening the Church of England and keeping foreign invaders at bay did not prevent her being vain enough to avoid having her portrait painted after her thirties.

Her Essex presence lingers on in tales of haunted dwellings. While still a princess, she had sheltered from the wrath of Mary in The Place, Great Bardfield, and her ghost has been 'seen' there. A more likely location for a sighting was at Horeham Hall, Thaxted. At the end of the nineteenth century, a groom from the hall, arriving home late, heard the distinct tapping of her high-heels and vowed never to be late home again. Nearly 300 years later, Elizabeth was feared in death as in life.

Thomasine Tyler

Sixteenth Century

As Thomasine was around – and infamous – in 1577, it is not surprising that there is little concrete information about her. She was not a royal, a royal mistress or a witch. But she is worth inclusion because of her description in the Sessions Rolls as a 'malefactor' and 'riotous person'.

Thomasine's name is prominent among thirty listed spinsters, all of 'Burntwood' (Brentwood) who were:

> unlawfully assembled in a certain place called Burntwood Chapel and in the steeple of the said chapel and around the churchyard of the same, and with force and arms they pulled a certain Richard Brooke, schoolmaster, out of the said chapel and locking themselves in the same, having and riotously using and bearing against the servants of . . . Wistan Browne (sheriff) and other King's subjects then present these arms, to wit five pitchforks, bills, a piked staff, two hot spits, three bows and nine arrows, one hatchet, one great hammer, hot water in two kettles, and a great sharp stone; and that they kept themselves in the said chapel until they were arrested and removed by . . . the sheriff and justices on the same day.

Wistan Browne claimed to be the owner of the thirteenth-century chapel (of St Thomas the Martyr) and had intended to demolish it to use the materials elsewhere on his estate. He had already sent wagons guarded by armed men to take away the pulpit and the pews. He was ready to remove the bell and the church clock but the townsfolk were outraged at his actions. They had delivered a petition to the Lord Keeper of the Great Seal which had been ignored.

It looks as if Richard Brooke had been seeking refuge in the sanctuary of the chapel, as would have been a common practice for those under attack, but his involvement is not clear. Thomasine and her angry lady

The thirteenth-century Chapel of St Thomas. (Courtesy of Father Bemand)

The remains of St Thomas Chapel, 2007. (Author's Collection)

friends took no heed of his attempt to escape their attentions. Their own attempt to hide after the attack was also to no avail, given the eventual intervention by the sheriff. Seventeen of the thirty spinsters escaped committal to gaol, and they had sympathy from local menfolk. John Mynto, a yeoman, refused to help in suppressing them when ordered to do so. There was also a Henry Dalley, a labourer, who attempted to rescue Thomasine from custody 'forcibly and with violence'. Those who did not escape were released on bail, and dealt with leniently when they came to trial, being fined four pence each.

The demonstration had the desired effect in that Wistan was ordered to appear before council and to 'forbeare the pulling downe of the chappell'. During the trial, Wistan was blamed as the 'chefest cause of the said force' and was ordered to restore the chapel to the people, a property which up to that point he had regarded as his own possession.

So a victory for Thomasine and her tribe of spinsters. Were they amazons as they have been described? Possibly. Were they angry? Definitely. Did they regard their cause as just? Obviously. The ruins of the original chapel can still be seen in Brentwood's High Street, but memories of feisty Thomasine Tyler are harder to trace.

Frances Rich

1560–?

This is a case of infamy as a result of rash behaviour and an outspoken temperament rather than as a result of any cruel acts. Frances was the daughter of the 3rd Lord Rich (later Earl of Warwick) who fell for Captain Thomas Cammock of Maldon, a widower twenty years older than she. Captain Thomas, her father's coachman, was obviously not regarded as a suitable husband by her father, and the couple decided to elope when on their way to Rochford Hall, her father's principal residence.

Thomas carried Frances on his horse to Fambridge Ferry where the ferry was on the other side of the River Crouch. As they were being pursued, they tried swimming for it through nearly half a mile of salt water, subject to a violent tide. Thomas, it seems,

Site of Fambridge Ferry, 2007. (Author's Collection)

Ancient Maldon. (Author's Collection)

advised Frances against the venture but she said she would 'live and die' with him and all three, including the horse, plunged into the icy waters. Half way across, the horse tried to turn around, distracted perhaps by the sound of the pursuing horses behind them, and it was not easy for the couple to keep him on course.

But they got to Maldon where they were, to quote the Essex historian Philip Morant, 'wedded [at All Saints' church] and bedded'. Some accounts give Lord Rich the leading role in the pursuit, which was abandoned at the riverside, but it is not clear whether it was he or his son who conceded defeat by telling the couple 'God Bless' because of the risks they had taken.

Certainly, Thomas Cammock is fondly remembered in Maldon. It was reputedly he who gave the town their first public water supply of piped water from a well on his pastureland. He also gave the borough a further gift of land, and maintained a pious façade. This 'Essex Lochinvar' was also regarded as having a swagger and an air of romance about him, making him attractive to women. His first wife, Ursula, gave him a family of four sons and five daughters, and Frances went on to have a further two sons and eleven daughters. Baptisms of thirteen of the children are entered in the All Saints' register, plus a number of burials.

Less is known about Frances than about Thomas. However, one incident in 1598 is recorded. There seems to have been an ongoing problem between the Cammock family and the Tuke family of Layer Marney. Allegedly, the Cammocks had a family pew at the church in Layer Marney which was on one occasion locked by the Tukes,

Cammock monument, All Saints' church, Maldon.
(Author's Collection)

Interior of All Saints' church, 2007.
(Author's Collection)

denying Frances and her children and servants access. Threats were issued by the Tukes, resulting in Frances, her ten-year-old daughter Martha and her manservant all being physically assaulted. Frances put up quite a violent resistance, it seems, tearing her lawn apron during the scuffle.

Thomas and two of his sons continued in the service of Robert Rich, and Thomas Junior remained in the family home at Maldon following his father's death in 1602. All twenty-five Cammocks – children, two wives, and Thomas – are portrayed in the alabaster and marble monument erected after Thomas's death on the east wall of the north aisle of All Saints' church. The monument was erected by the children in their father's memory and is still an impressive focal point with arms and escutcheons clearly visible. However, both wives look identical, so it is impossible to form an impression of Frances's appearance.

When Thomas died, it is even more difficult to track Frances. She seems to have moved to London with some of her younger children, joined at some stage by Thomas Junior. The latter son, after marrying, voyaged to North America, and died in 1643 during a further voyage to Bermuda. Did she live a long and vigorous life in the capital? If you know, the author would love to hear!

Postcript: A coral necklace alleged to have been worn by Frances Rich when she eloped was displayed by Rochford Council at an exhibition in 1955 as part of the Rochford Jubilee, but has mysteriously disappeared since.

Lady Penelope Rich

1563–1607

After spending her childhood at Chartley, near Stafford, the principal seat of her father's family, Penelope (the great-granddaughter of Mary Boleyn), and her youngest siblings were moved by her widowed mother to stay with relatives in different parts of the country. Although her mother had the option of the Bennington estate on the Hertfordshire–Essex border as part of her husband's will, she seems to have preferred to stay with other members of her prosperous family, reducing her responsibility and increasing male input. Eleven of Penelope's sixteen siblings survived into adulthood and several were already married by the time Lettice, her mother, remarried in 1578. Her new step-father was Robert, Earl of Leicester, Queen Elizabeth's favourite.

Interestingly, this marriage, at Wanstead in 1581, was not revealed to the queen even though she visited Wanstead soon after. When she did find out, a year later, Lettice's court career ended, although Penelope was tolerated, even encouraged.

Penelope caused quite a stir at court in 1581 with her outstanding beauty and musical skills. Philip Sidney, the poet, is said to have immortalised her as Stella in his poems, first published in 1591. As a member of Elizabeth's team of ladies, she was now in the best of all marriage markets, but Elizabeth did not encourage the ladies of the court to marry. This may have been in part due to jealousy but in part it was also due to her liking of power and control.

However, when the Huntingdon family, acting as Penelope's guardians, sought permission for her to marry the man who had inherited the title of the second richest landowner in the country, Elizabeth gave her approval. Perhaps Elizabeth didn't mind the idea of Penelope marrying someone without any claims on the throne, especially someone who was a radical Protestant.

The lucky man was Baron Robert Rich of Leighs Priory, north of Chelmsford. Lord Rich had recently inherited many Essex manors, including Leighs, Wanstead and Rochford, bought by his father from Henry VIII when the king was selling off monastery land. So his financial position and his youth would have, in Penelope's eyes, offset the lack of refinement inherited from his infamously corrupt father. Philip Sidney was in no way such a good 'catch'. She certainly continued as Sidney's muse, perhaps his lover, although the latter is difficult to prove.

Leighs was, by all accounts, a stunning residence, perfectly located for hunting in the local forests. It was a converted Augustinian priory, the great hall formerly the nave and the family chapel formerly the chapter house. There was a towering gatehouse, a dairy, brewhouse, ponds, a bowling green, private gardens and stables, surrounded by

Portrait of Penelope Rich. (Courtesy of Lambeth Palace Library)

wild parkland. Penelope also made frequent visits to Rochford Hall, the home of her mother-in-law, and formerly owned by Mary Boleyn.

Penelope gave birth to two daughters in the early 1580s, named Lettice and, unusually, Essex. Essex may well have been named after her favourite brother Robert, Earl of Essex (who was of course soon to be Queen Elizabeth's young lover). Her first son, Robert, was born at Wanstead, her mother's home, in 1587, taking the name of his father – and her brother.

The queen persuaded Essex to buy Wanstead House from his mother who was still trying to sort out Leicester's debts after his death even though she had married for the third time. The deal did finally go through after a lot of wrangling between mother and son. Wanstead was seen to be a fitting country estate for Elizabeth's favourite. In the meantime, Penelope was busy having her portrait painted.

Once Penelope had given birth to a second son (an heir and a spare) she was not happy spending so much time at Leighs, although she returned often for the sake of her husband and children. The marriage to Robert Rich had been relatively happy, but it had started out as – and stayed – a marriage of convenience. She spent more time at court, and more time with Sir Charles Blount, an old friend with a taste for fine books and wine. Their affair was protracted, but discreet.

Penelope also spent time with her brother's new family at Wanstead. She was far more successful at entertaining diplomats and royals than her shyer, less confident

Undated print of Leighs Priory. (Author's Collection)

sister-in-law. It was an ideal location for hunting in Waltham Forest and its forty acres had been substantially improved over the years, with splendid guest quarters set around a quadrangle.

When Penelope admitted to her husband that she was expecting Charles's baby, Lord Rich had family honour to consider and seems to have been able to accept the position he was in – perhaps for love of his wife. She continued to support her husband in public and they preserved a united front. Penelope and Charles continued their affair in secret, at his town house or at Wanstead. Lord Rich could not have predicted that another four children would follow.

During the plague year of 1593, Penelope took her mother, sister Dorothy, pregnant sister-in-law Frances and other womenfolk in her circle to Leighs for safety. Once the outbreak was over, she was free again to revert to spending more time in Wanstead and London. Penelope built up quite a cult following at Essex House, her brother's home in The Strand, his relationship with the queen having a positive spin on Penelope's popularity. She became the subject not only of sonnets and portraits but of popular love songs and flirty dances – even the 'Dark Lady' of Shakespeare's sonnets has been argued to be Penelope Rich.

After the failure of Essex in an expedition to intercept the Spanish treasure fleet off the Azores, his popularity was on the wane, with enemies at court and his myriad of affairs becoming less acceptable as the women he chose became closer and closer to Elizabeth's circle. At the same time, he and the queen had started to argue about political issues and he was becoming disillusioned with a life controlled by a shallow woman who was now elderly, holding little attraction for him.

William Shakespeare, one of several men inspired by Lady Penelope. (Author's Collection)

When someone was needed as Lord Deputy of Ireland, a role for which Charles, now Lord Mountjoy, was a contender, Elizabeth seems to have manipulated the situation in favour of Essex. To finance his campaign, however, he was told to sell Wanstead. Because of Penelope's fondness for it, Mountjoy bought it from him for £4,300. This was the first property Mountjoy had owned, but the transaction was not a victory for Penelope, who did not want her brother in danger in Ireland.

Back in Leighs with her husband, she received news that Essex had returned without permission, storming into the queen's bedchamber when she was wigless, resulting in his arrest. He had not been able to handle Ireland, and Mountjoy was his replacement. But Mountjoy was in touch with King James of Scotland who was making a bid for the throne of England, urging James to action. Essex and Penelope were behind him.

Although Essex was released (stripped of title and income), and Mountjoy despatched to Ireland, the communications with James continued. Essex had nothing to lose by attempting a controlling coup with the support of several hundred Londoners.

The attempt failed dismally and Penelope stayed to help him destroy damning evidence at Essex House. When soldiers arrived to arrest Essex, Penelope too was detained and named as among the ringleaders, the only female conspirator. Robert and the other conspirators were beheaded. Penelope, devastated by her brother's death, escaped such retribution, but it seems that even her lawful husband was no longer behind her.

When King James came to the English throne in 1603 on Elizabeth's death, Penelope and her lover – back from doing a good job in Ireland – rose to royal favour. Mountjoy was given the title of Earl of Devonshire, and Master of the Ordnance. Penelope became lady-in-waiting to the new queen, Anne. They were both too busy, however, to spend much time together in Wanstead.

Once the peace with Spain was signed, they had more opportunity to enjoy the estate with its walled grounds, formal gardens and heronry. Mountjoy was able to build up his library before returning to Ireland, creating a valuable and famous collection. She was still a renowned beauty, by now in her forties, and building up her influence again at court. The fact that she had been living openly with Mountjoy in Wanstead House had ruffled no royal feathers, being the acceptable face of noble marriages at the time. However, when the gunpowder plot shook the court, and the country, Penelope was quietly divorcing Lord Rich, the father of her eldest four children (the younger five were fathered by Mountjoy/Devonshire).

This move, ironically, led to a downturn in her fortunes. In spite of the disgrace that divorce meant at court, she and Lord Rich cooperated in the action. Contemporary divorce conditions provided that the couple should now remain celibate and not remarry during the lifetime of the other. Penelope completely ignored such unwelcome stipulations, and married Devonshire in a modest ceremony at Wanstead House with the help of a sympathetic chaplain.

The sanctimonious King James was less sympathetic. Although he had no objection to adultery, he did not like public admission of such behaviour. He was also appalled at such a deliberate flouting of the law and saw it as a challenge to his own divine authority. The chaplain, Laud, was severely censured for the part he had played – although he went on to become Archbishop of Canterbury. As for Penelope, she was banished from the royal court. Devonshire escaped because his presence was needed at the gunpowder plot trials. The ceremony had, incidentally, not legitimised their children, but it did mean that Devonshire could make a will in their favour and he pleaded eloquently with the king for legal recognition of their marriage, to no avail.

After just three months of marriage, Devonshire died in London, aged just forty-four, his pregnant wife at his side. His health had been deteriorating for a while, not helped by the disgrace of his marriage and his bitterness at James's reaction. His heavy smoking, a recent habit – thanks to Sir Walter Raleigh – could have been a contributory factor. Although his victories in Ireland earned him a state funeral, the scramble started for his fortune. Unsurprisingly Devonshire's kinsmen fought the will which favoured Penelope and her family. Her subsequent miscarriage gave them the opportunity of suggesting that she had faked her condition to persuade Devonshire to make such a will. Criminal proceedings were launched against her at the Court of the Star Chamber to answer charges of forgery. No punches were pulled in court, where she was described as a harlot, concubine, whore and adulteress. Her only concession was to abandon her claim to Devonshire's titles.

In July 1607, before the legal case against her had concluded, Penelope was dead. She, too, was just forty-four. The circumstances, and even the location, are unclear. Possible complications from her miscarriage are just one possibility. The final resting place of one of the most notorious beauties in the history of Essex is also unknown. She had managed a life of spirit, independence and adventure despite all the restrictions placed on women at the end of the sixteenth century.

The only remaining portrait of Penelope is at Lambeth Palace, allegedly placed there by Archbishop Laud as a reminder of his 'sin' in performing what he considered an illegal marriage between her and Charles Blount. She displays a bold expression which serves to underline her individuality.

Frances Howard, Countess of Somerset

1590–1632

The mansion of Audley End in Saffron Walden was built as the largest private dwelling in England, inspired by engravings of a French chateau. This grand dwelling in five acres was the imposing home for many years of Thomas Howard, an Elizabethan seaman and nobleman, and his second wife Catherine. Frances, their second daughter, had as many as twelve siblings.

Frances Howard.
(Author's Collection)

As with so many women born into rich families, Frances's marriage at age sixteen was an arranged match. Her husband was Robert Devereux, 3rd Earl of Essex, son of Elizabeth's favourite, even younger than she was. Because of their youth, sexual intercourse was postponed while Robert travelled overseas but when he returned, after three years, he seems to have been unable to consummate the marriage. During the summer of 1610, Frances spent the summer with her parents at Audley End while Essex divided his time between Saffron Walden and his estate in Staffordshire (Chartley).

Unsurprisingly, the marriage deteriorated, and Frances was linked firstly with Prince Henry who died in 1612 at the age of eighteen, and then with Robert Carr. The latter was an even better prospect politically for the Howard family than Essex, as Carr was a favourite of James I. In May 1613, therefore, Frances petitioned for an annulment, and suffered the indignity of being 'inspected' to confirm her virginity. There was a problem with the annulment, however, because Devereux claimed that he was not impotent with other women, only with Frances. This idea of selective impotency was difficult to explain, and it took four months, and the intervention of King James, before the annulment was granted.

While waiting, Carr had been ably assisted by his friend, the poet and essayist Sir Thomas Overbury. Thomas composed his love letters for him – but was in actuality not keen on a marriage between the two and this hostility eventually alienated the two friends. Carr was instrumental in Overbury's imprisonment in the Tower of London when the latter refused a mission to Russia, which was allegedly an act of disobedience to the King. However, Frances felt he had not gone far enough. She regarded Overbury's attitude as a threat to the happiness of her proposed marriage to Carr. Certainly, she and Overbury were mutually antagonistic – Overbury called her a 'filthy, base woman' and she regarded him as 'scum' and the 'devil incarnate'. She is reputed to have offered Sir David Wood a thousand pounds to assassinate this devil, but Wood refused.

In September, Overbury died – apparently of consumption or some other common disease – and the annulment was finally granted. Frances married Robert Carr a few months later in an extravagant celebration that disregarded law and religion, but the damage was done in any case. She was publicly portrayed as the villain of the piece, because fans of Essex felt that she had in fact rebuffed and betrayed him. The evidence of her virginity was discredited by court wits and poets, who suggested that another woman had been examined in Frances's place.

Worse was to come for this particular Essex girl. In 1615, a lieutenant of the Tower, Sir Gervase Elwes, claimed that he had thwarted a plot to kill Overbury during the annulment hearings. He named Richard Weston as the attempted poisoner, but, under interrogation, also implicated Countess Frances and her friend Anne Turner, a doctor's widow. It seems that Frances had tried repeatedly to have Overbury poisoned, with the help of Anne and other accomplices. Poisoned wine, tarts and jellies were all sent into the Tower, most intercepted by Elwes. Frances also acquired drugs from a notorious apothecary and from a satanic potion-maker, and bribed her servants to mix them with Overbury's food. He was finally finished off in September 1613 with a poisoned enema. It doesn't get much nastier than that.

At Weston's subsequent trial, it was Frances who was the most vilified. She was described variously as a whore, a witch and a syphilitic sorceress who had crippled

Audley End. (Author's Collection)

Essex's manhood and killed Overbury. By choosing poison as her 'weapon', she had chosen a method alien to the English character and resultantly abhorrent. In Henry VIII's reign, those guilty of poisoning were subjected to death by being boiled in hot water.

As for Frances, she confessed before trial in 1616 and King James spared her life because of her confession and penitence. Carr, the Earl of Somerset, had also been accused and imprisoned but he denied any involvement in what had happened to Overbury. Although he too was spared, the couple spent a further five-and-a-half years in the Tower. Only the innocent Elwes was sent to the gallows after an unfair trial.

Anne, daughter of the Carrs, was born in the Tower in 1615. She was taken to Audley End and brought up there. It is not known if Frances returned to the family seat in Saffron Walden after her release in 1621, but she certainly returned there after contracting ovarian cancer (or possibly a variation of the same disease) and was buried there in 1632. Her cancer was regarded at the time as an appropriate 'punishment' for her crime.

Ann Carter

d. 1629

For a change, this was a woman with no power or authority, and indeed a woman who challenged those who had these advantages, which were not always used to benefit the working classes. Little is known of her life before her marriage in 1620 to butcher John Carter from Maldon – apart from her maiden name, Barrington.

One of her first recorded clashes is with the Church. She was questioned in 1623 as to why she was not at church, replying that if someone was provided to do her work she would indeed attend. A year later she was able to prevent the arrest of her husband – no doubt for a similarly unlikely 'offence' – by the use of a cudgel against the sergeant-at-arms.

More famously, however, it was Ann Carter who deemed herself 'captain' of a large crowd of women who protested over the export of grain in 1629. They were not the only ones who were against such exports when local populations faced hunger, partly as a result of rising food prices. The angry crowd marched to where a Flemish ship was loading the rye and 'forced' the sailors to load it into the women's aprons and bonnets instead. Ann had particular cause for anger as she had already been hauled up in court for infringing market regulations – while foreign merchants were allowed to trade, unchecked and on a grand scale.

Such a level of rioting was not just a reaction to starvation – it was also the culmination of ongoing exchanges between the poor and the authorities, and was planned as a form of coercion to remedy the deprivation that the rioters were experiencing. In the short term, the riot had some effect as grain was purchased for distribution to the poor at favourable rates, a result that the rioters had fought for.

Two months later, Ann rode through the region collecting support for another grievance. A local baker assisted her by writing letters – indicating that Ann herself was illiterate. This time, she was leading a crowd of unemployed textile workers, an industry struggling due to foreign competition and the closure of foreign markets, especially as a result of the war with Spain. Spinners, weavers and carders, mainly from the weaving towns of Witham, Bocking and Braintree, were all thrown out of work. They responded in their hundreds to her rally cry of 'Come my brave lads of Maulden . . . we will not starve', giving them enough force not only to attack ships taking on grain with more violence against the crews, but also to break into a grain store and steal a large amount of grain. One story credits them with kidnapping a chief merchant called Gamble at Heybridge Dock, and ransoming him for £20.

The riots seem to have taken place at Borough Hills, an isolated area on the edge of the marshland where Maldon's water bailiff collected the tolls. So far as Maldon

Canal near Maldon. (Author's Collection)

was concerned, the disturbances involved mostly outsiders whose rioting occurred on the boundary of its territory. Ann Carter's role, however, was of more than peripheral importance.

Because of her involvement in two riots within three months, Ann had gone too far, especially given the political instability of the reign of Charles I. Two riots in quick succession smacked of rebellion against the government. Alleged ringleaders – eight of them – were arrested and interrogated and a special judicial commission sat to execute justice just one week later. Three male rioters and Captain Ann Carter were found guilty and hanged the next day, 30 May. Although Ann probably had children, because keeping the children fed was the main path to hunger for so many families, her family situation would have been irrelevant. She was the only woman hanged in that period for a food riot, even though such riots were inevitably female-dominated.

Since her execution, many have tried to establish whether she – and other female rioters – were acting independently or at the instigation of their menfolk, but nothing has been proven. Although her age at death is not known, she was almost certainly a young woman, but was she a well-meaning woman, challenging authority at the wrong time and in the wrong place, or someone who courted violence . . . you decide.

Margaret Cavendish, Duchess of Newcastle

c. 1623–73

This Essex eccentric was born Margaret Lucas at St John's Abbey, then near and now in, Colchester. She was the youngest child of Thomas and Elizabeth Lucas – and her mother also merits a brief mention as having had an illegitimate son by Thomas at a time (1597) when he had been banished for duelling and unable to return to England to marry her. Their marriage finally took place when James I came to the throne.

The abbey and estate had been bought by Margaret's grandfather following the dissolution of the monasteries, and the family – and home – were prominent in the

Margaret Cavendish.
(Courtesy of Essex Record Office)

St John's Abbey, Colchester.
(Author's Collection)

area. The Lucases lived half the year in Colchester and half the year in London. Her father died when she was only two, and she was probably spoiled by her liberal mother and older siblings.

Margaret's education was at the hands of private tutors, and, although rudimentary, was extensive by the standards of lesser female mortals at the time. Apart from reading and writing, she learned singing, dancing, playing music and needlework. The latter skill was responsible for the bizarre velvet dresses she took to designing and wearing. As to her literary skill, Margaret had written a number of books by the age of twelve, none of which appear to have been published.

As a teenager, however, this idyllic life was upturned by the dangers of civil war, and Margaret went to live in Oxford with her sister, Catherine, in 1642, where she was introduced into court circles and accompanied the queen into exile in Paris in 1644. This is where she met William Cavendish, Marquis of Newcastle, a widower, some thirty years her senior, the man she married in 1645. Cavendish was considered an attractive man and regarded as a hero despite a defeat by Cromwell when he was commander at Marston Moor. He does not seem to have been deterred by Margaret's outfits or her love of philosophical debate, and is known to have found her generous figure particularly entrancing.

The couple seemingly idolised each other, and they travelled happily between England and Antwerp for a number of years. Although her husband had many of his estates confiscated by Parliament, leaving him in financial difficulties, she supported him and they entertained lavishly, ignoring such inconsequential details.

By 1653, Margaret had established herself as having an eccentric sense of dress which bore no relation to current fashions, and an eccentric attitude to life, once being described as less 'sober' than people in Bedlam, the mental institution. She also developed an argumentative approach to philosophy, especially after her Royalist brother Charles was condemned for treason and executed by firing squad in 1648, following the siege of Colchester. This siege included a Parliamentarian attack on the Lucas family home, causing considerable damage.

This was the period when Margaret started writing plays and poetry, such as the memorable 'What is liquid?':

> All that doth flow we cannot liquid name
> Or else would fire and water be the same;
> But that is liquid which is moist and wet
> Fire that property can never get
> Then 'tis not cold that doth the fire put out.
> But 'tis the wet that makes it die, no doubt.

Her first book of poetry was published in 1653, and it seems she began to take an interest in publishing more of her work to avoid total oblivion after death. The couple settled back in England when Charles II came back to the throne in 1660, and Newcastle's estates were restored. Margaret continued to write poetry, plays, essays and memoirs. None of her work was revised or corrected, as Margaret is said to have preferred making to 'mending'.

The duchess's status saw to it that plenty of people flattered her and her work. Samuel Pepys was more honest, however, and described her poetry as the most ridiculous thing 'that ever was wrote'. John Evelyn, another contemporary diarist, described her as a 'mighty pretender'. Latterly, Virginia Woolf has described her as having 'futile' philosophies, 'intolerable' plays, 'dull' verses, while conceding that 'there is something noble and high-spirited as well as crack-brained and bird-witted' in her writing! Margaret's plays were once – though no longer perhaps – considered 'unactable' and her husband, writing plays in retirement, had more success with this genre than his wife. Margaret's plays are, for the most part, unconnected scenes, full of lengthy soliloquies, with characters embodying vice or virtue, bereft of wit and humour.

Her appearance also provoked widespread comment especially on her visits to London, as did her risqué jokes and colourful oaths. Samuel Pepys, again, compared her to Queen Kristina of Sweden, known for her cross-dressing, and made reference to the black patches on her face which served to disguise 'pimples'. Sir Charles Lyttleton met Margaret when she was 'dressed in a vest' and Mary Evelyn (John's wife) described her as extravagant and vain. One particular velvet cap was decorated with long feathers obscuring her face. It does seem she had something to be vain about, however, as she was apparently a physically attractive woman throughout her life.

Margaret's fiction output was a tad racy for its time. *Assaulted and Pursued Chastity*, for example, features the Prince of Sensuality chasing the Lady Affectionata along with other lusty young men. In the more hot-blooded of her published works, she often favoured adultery and seduction, and the frontispiece often added to their titillation by promoting her well-developed bosom in a low-cut gown.

Domestically, it seems that she tried, and failed, to cook, bake and preserve, leaving this to her housekeeper. Having a generally clumsy nature, she also never managed to learn how to spin, although she had a small flock of sheep. At some stage she became known as Mad Madge of Newcastle, but this name may have been a posthumous one. She died at the marital home in Nottinghamshire and was buried at Westminster Abbey. There were no children from the marriage, but Margaret does not seem to have regretted this deficiency. She is quoted as saying that 'women hazard their lives by bringing children into the world and hath the greatest share of trouble in bringing them up'. Not so mad perhaps?

Postscript: The one literary work which has stood up to the test of time is the biography of her husband, *The Life of William Cavendish*.

Abigail Masham (née Hill)

c. 1670–1734

It is inevitable that there are more infamous women in the upper echelons than in the lower – not because the 'lower classes' were more responsible citizens or more law-abiding (far from it), but because more records were kept about those with courtly connections. Sad but true.

Abigail certainly does not seem to have been high born, although distant family members had royal connections. Her story is of someone who altered the course of history through her disruptive effect on Sarah, the Duchess of Marlborough. When Abigail's merchant father went bankrupt, she had to accept a menial position with a distant relative, although still very young. Her story really begins when she is rescued from a menial position in the household of this relative, Lady Rivers, and taken into the home of her rich cousin, Sarah Churchill, in high favour at the court of Princess Anne. When a place as bedchamber woman in the princess's household became vacant, Sarah proposed her cousin Abigail for the position, a suggestion readily accepted.

At the beginning of the eighteenth century, Abigail was regarded as the most influential of Queen Anne's personal servants after the Duchess of Marlborough, the latter beginning to have political differences of opinion with her mistress. Abigail, as a result of her own political interests, began having evening meetings with Robert Harley, a passionate Whig parliamentarian known as Robin the Trickster. It was he who realised how useful Abigail's influence could be. It was said to be Harley who persuaded Samuel Masham, an army officer, that marriage to the poor and plain Abigail (nicknamed 'Carbuncles') could be equally advantageous. Samuel, the son of a baronet, came from a comfortable home, Otes Manor, at High Laver near Harlow. It seems that he had taken little convincing by Harley. In fact, he is said to have told his family that he was in love with Abigail.

Abigail Masham. (Author's Collection)

The 1707 ceremony was conducted in the presence of the queen, who presented Abigail with a substantial cash dowry. Sarah does not appear to have been invited to the wedding. On discovering the queen's collusion in her cousin's marriage, Sarah decided that this was the reason that the queen was no longer listening to her (Sarah's) political advice. She obviously thought of Abigail's influence as underhand and unnatural, and began slandering her, taking up suggestions that had been whispered in the court as to Abigail's susceptibility to women and younger men. The queen took this as a personal attack and Sarah was ostracised as a result.

Abigail continued to support Harley politically, and used her influence to give him secret access to the queen. She also managed to secure a powerful army post for her brother John, Harley instructing the Duke of Marlborough in this regard, which meant that both Marlboroughs now mistrusted Abigail's influence and tried to remove her from court. They failed, and Sarah felt obliged to resign her court position.

Otes, near Harlow. (Courtesy of Essex Record Office)

The power Abigail had at court increased when she was given the post of keeper of the privy purse in 1711. She was authorised to draw money from Hoare's Bank and issue royal receipts. No records remain which detail whether such transactions were totally honest. Either way, it must have been a tempting situation for someone of her background.

Her five children were born between 1708 and 1714, but she maintained contact with Harley throughout these years, although technically he no longer needed her services as such. Jonathan Swift, the author, was quite an admirer of Abigail's political acumen, and would have noticed that she gradually switched her allegiance from Harley (now Earl of Oxford) to Bolingbroke, Harley's rival. Accusations that Bolingbroke bribed Abigail were made by Harley's family, so must be taken with a pinch of salt.

Harley's dismissal (Queen Anne wrote to Jonathan Swift in regard to Harley's drink problem and lack of reliability) followed by Anne's death left Abigail out in the cold. She was apparently accused of stealing some of the queen's jewellery – although even her acquired enemy Sarah protested that she was the only person that Abigail had ever robbed. From now on, Abigail spent time in obscurity rather than at court, and she moved to Otes in 1723 when Sir Francis, Samuel's father, died. Incidentally, another famous 'death' at Otes only nineteen years earlier was that of the philosopher John Locke, an asthmatic. He was a tenant of Sir Francis, paying one pound per week to escape the London air.

From unpromising beginnings, therefore, Abigail, although now without her influence, could look back on a time when she had been ready to risk alienating the Queen of England in order to achieve her personal and political ends. She does not come across as a flighty female looking to advance more shallow interests. More significantly, she almost certainly had a hand in shaping important policies, with her consistent advocacy of the Jacobites.

Abigail died of an unknown illness in 1734 at Otes, and is buried in High Laver church. Her husband survived her for over twenty years as a brigadier and an MP. The house was demolished more than a century ago, but a phantom carriage is still said to drive through the village carrying a sad female figure. Little else of solidity survives except in Sarah's vindictive letters and Jonathan (later Dean) Swift's contemporary written comments. It is said that she was, in fact, more literate than Sarah, but she took care not to put anything in writing that might be kept – especially if it could reveal anything unsavoury about her behaviour.

Catherine (Kitty) Canham

1720–52

A short life, but a memorable one. This is the story of a heart-breaker born in the parish of Beaumont-cum-Moze adjoining Thorpe-le-Soken. Her parents, Robert and Judith, ran a prosperous farm, but Kitty seems to have been the only one of their children that lived to adulthood. It was a sign of the times that, in 1729, two brothers died, Bartholomew (aged four) and Robert (seven), Kitty being just nine. The family's home was an imposing early Tudor manor house with red Elizabethan gables – Beaumont Hall – on a high hill with sloping fields overlooking the creek.

Legend has it that young Kitty was fascinating and beautiful, with plenty of admirers. The lucky man whose suit was encouraged was the Reverend Alexander Henry Gough, an educated man, older than Kitty. Alexander asked his younger brother, Maurice, also a cleric, for his opinion as to Kitty, and Maurice is alleged to have indicated that she was 'a beautiful creature who will play you a trick'.

If this was supposed to put Alexander off, it had no effect, for the couple were married in the little local church after a brief courtship, making their home in Thorpe. There are no indications that she cared for her husband, but she would have certainly felt under pressure to marry. The reverend did not care for entertaining or for society, and when Kitty defied him by attending a ball, there would be quite an argument upon her return. Perhaps it was predictable that a quiet life as a parson's wife in such rural surroundings was not suited to someone as young and lively as Kitty. One day in 1748, the disillusioned beauty literally disappeared from the vicarage.

Portrait of Kitty Canham. (From a replica drawing by the author)

Different sources give varying accounts of her disappearance. One indicates that she made a trip to London to consult a doctor, but did not return afterwards. Another suggests she disappeared from a masquerade with a mystery companion. Whatever the truth, she managed to get away, and was never heard of in Thorpe again until her body was returned for her funeral.

Our bored Essex wife had 'married' Lord Dalmeny in London. Where and when they met remains a mystery – possibly in one of London's assembly rooms – but she obviously led him to believe she was single. Historically, no one has indicated that Lord Dalmeny was part of any mutual conspiracy to commit bigamy.

The couple, apparently devoted, travelled widely in Europe for a number of years. They enjoyed a prosperous, adventurous existence which should have satisfied Kitty's apparent craving for adventure and excitement. However, the opposite seems to have happened. Kitty began a process of decline. Whether this was an undiagnosed illness is impossible to ascertain after so many years. This does seem to be the most likely explanation.

But this is not the explanation handed down over the centuries. As her body became frail, this seems to have been blamed on the guilt she was feeling. Certainly, as she approached the end, she felt remorse for her actions, and regretted the way she had treated Alexander Gough. On her deathbed, in the beautiful city of Verona, Kitty signalled for pencil and paper, being incapable of speech. The words she wrote were:

> I am the wife of the Reverend Alexander Gough, Vicar of
> Thorpe-le-Soken, in Essex. My maiden name was Catherine Canham.
> My last request is to be buried at Thorpe.

This final effort was the last that Kitty was able to make. Lord Dalmeny was obviously horrified, although he must have wondered if this was some kind of dying hallucination. Even so, he determined to carry out her dying wish.

Kitty's body was embalmed and laid in a handsome, silver-plated coffin, enclosed in an ordinary wooden case for travelling. Her clothes and jewellery were packed into chests and Lord Dalmeny set out on his sad journey across Europe. He was reluctant to draw attention to himself or his macabre luggage. This may have been part of the reason he gave a false name when reaching the French coast, in order to engage a ship to Dover with no questions asked about the case he was 'exporting'.

From Dover, he took a second ship to Harwich, but the winds drove the vessel down the River Colne, near to the town of Hythe, where the customs authorities took quite an interest in the wooden container. Imagining that it contained smuggled goods, an officer prepared to plunge his cutlass into it until Lord Dalmeny, purporting to be a merchant, drew his sword and told them that his wife was inside. This made things, if anything, look even worse for him, as now murder was suspected, not helped when they opened the chests to find them full of jewellery and splendid dresses. The coffin was opened and conveyed to St Leonard's church on Hythe Hill, where it was left exposed in the vestry for identification. For want of a better prison, the grieving Lord Dalmeny was also detained in the church. He spent several days by the side of his lost love, viewed by a number of curious strangers, still keeping his identity a secret from the authorities.

Eventually, someone who had known Kitty as Kitty Gough approached Lord Dalmeny with his suspicions and, sensing a sympathetic listener, the prisoner admitted that he was trying to carry out her last wishes, and gave his name and a full account of the events that had brought him to Essex. The Reverend Gough, on hearing the news, threatened to run Lord Dalmeny through his body – an unusual reaction for a member of the clergy.

It seems that the two 'husbands' came face to face beside the body of Kitty in Hythe vestry. Gough wanted to identify her, and Dalmeny refused to leave her. The meeting must have been extraordinary, but it seems they parted on good terms with mutual sympathy.

Left: St Michael's church, Thorpe-le-Soken, 2007. (Author's Collection)

Below: The Bell Inn, Thorpe-le-Soken, 2007. (Author's Collection)

Just a few days later, one of the most elaborate funerals of the time was seen entering Thorpe-le-Soken from the Colchester road. The silver coffin was carried on a magnificent hearse, drawn by black-plumed horses, with mourners muffled in crêpe and silk following, including Dalmeny. On reaching the vicarage, Lord Dalmeny alighted from his coach and went to fetch the Reverend Gough so that they could both follow Kitty to her last resting place, by the side of her brothers in the vault of St Michael's church.

It seems that the Canham family tomb was removed when the church was largely rebuilt at the end of the nineteenth century. Part of the tomb's structure was used to pave the entrance to the porch, and cut to fit, with little of the remaining inscription – if any – now legible.

A portrait was painted of Kitty, probably before her first marriage. This oil, or a copy of it, was hung in Beaumont Hall and then for some time in the lounge of the Bell Hotel in the High Street, Thorpe-le-Soken, adjoining the church. It was one of the few surviving artefacts following a fire there in 1999 but it is not clear as to where it is now. It seems that several people have experienced the sensation of a presence in one of the guest bedrooms there, and seen a shadowy female figure, before and after the fire and refurbishment. Such is the stuff of legend.

On a more practical note, neither 'widower' remarried. Lord Dalmeny died in 1755, aged just thirty-one, and the Reverend Gough stayed in Thorpe until his death in 1774.

Elizabeth Jeffryes

1727–52

Although born in Shropshire, Elizabeth was sent to live with her uncle Joseph in Walthamstow, then part of Essex, when she was five years old. Joseph was childless but had acquired a considerable fortune as a butcher, and he raised her as his own daughter and made her heiress to the bulk of his estate.

The situation changed when Elizabeth was a shapely and fresh-complexioned young woman in her early twenties. She became involved with one of her uncle's servants, John Swan, and may have become pregnant by him. Whether pregnant or not, Joseph threatened to alter his will and cut her off as he did not approve of the relationship. It seems that her continued good behaviour was a condition of her inheritance. As a result, Elizabeth and John began planning her uncle's murder.

They initially approached Thomas Matthews, a gardener who had worked on the Jeffryes estate, a man with an unsavoury reputation. The couple gave him enough money for a 'brace of pistols' – around half a guinea – which he spent on drink. It seems that even he baulked at committing murder in spite of the £700 he was offered – a substantial amount in 1751.

When he turned up to meet them, without the pistols, Elizabeth 'damned him' as a villain, and Swan asked him to sign an agreement not to divulge their arrangement. Swan then took matters into his own hands – along with a loaded pistol which he had obviously acquired in case of just this eventuality, possibly from his master. Just

Undated print of old Walthamstow. (Author's Collection)

minutes later, Elizabeth jumped from her bedroom window, dressed only in her 'shift', rousing the neighbourhood with cries of 'Murder! Thieves!' Swan also emerged, seemingly disturbed by her outcry. Joseph Jeffryes was found in bed, with a gunshot to his head and a knife gash to his throat, apparently the victim of a break-in. The murderous couple had hid some plate, along with some pewter, brass and silver in a sack at the bottom of the stairs to support this theory.

The first person to be apprehended was Elizabeth, as there was no sign of a forced entry. She implicated Matthews, who gave a full account of events, in spite of the signed 'agreement'. Swan and Elizabeth were arrested and imprisoned. Their trials took place eight months later at Chelmsford Assizes in March 1752. Swan was accused not only of murder but also of what was then known as 'petty treason', and Elizabeth was accused of being an accessory. Matthews was the principal witness for the prosecution. The verdict in both cases was guilty, and Elizabeth only then made an interesting confession. She admitted that she had been plotting her uncle's death since she found him in bed with a maid and suspected that the maid would inherit what should have been hers. She also claimed that she had been 'debauched' by her uncle at the age of fifteen, resulting in two pregnancies – one miscarried, and one aborted with his help.

However, in subsequent accounts of Elizabeth's life, these claims are given little credence. She has been described variously as 'willing to prostitute' herself, as being of a 'vicious and wicked inclination' and as a grasping, treacherous individual who had enticed Swan to commit the crime. One story gives an account of her accusing a captain of the 'Second Regiment of Foot' of 'ravishing' her, the captain's version being that she was more than willing to grant 'favours'.

Thanks to the growing popularity of the broadsheet, and such early publications as the *London Evening Post*, the *Daily Advertiser* and *Read's Weekly Journal*, there is also an insight to her behaviour in prison when it appears that she was known to gamble, drink excessively and use plenty of profane language. She was also said to have worn inappropriately expensive slippers, shoes and elaborate dresses – and even to have talked about riding a pretty mare out of Chelmsford when she was acquitted, showing misplaced confidence.

Elizabeth's public face, however, was frail and vulnerable. It seems that

Broadsheet of Elizabeth Jeffryes' trial (note the wrong date). (University of Virginia Library)

she would have made a good career on the stage – fainting and swooning to order and falling into 'fits' at her trial. The day before her execution she apparently asked for her bespoke all-black coffin to be brought to her to check it for size.

The two convicted felons left Chelmsford gaol at four o'clock in the morning on 28 March 1752. She was in a cart, probably sitting on her own coffin, accompanied by the hangman. At some stage during the procession, she asked for a religious book and someone loaned her a copy of *Practice of True Devotion* – though how she managed to read this while fettered is a puzzle. Swan was drawn along behind, tied to a sledge. He accepted a little wine at Brentwood, but Elizabeth only drank water with 'hartshorn drops'. (Hartshorn was a precursor to baking powder, used to fend off fainting fits.)

Epping Forest. (Author's Collection)

The journey to the gallows 'beyond the Obelisk' at Epping Forest, some twenty-three miles away, took over eight hours. At every village en route, crowds of people lined the rough roads. Accompanying the unhappy pair were a troop of javelin men and a full convoy led by the Under Sheriff of Essex, such was the importance of public hangings. Local people would have wanted to see justice carried out, and the double execution attracted a large crowd. Wooden stands were erected and hired out to spectators in the usual contemporary fashion and people arrived on horseback, in coaches and on foot for the event. Incidentally, it should be borne in mind that Epping Forest covered a much greater area than it does now, and the area where the gallows was located is now built up.

On the one hand, Elizabeth was able to deny John Swan a farewell kiss when they were reunited on the gallows, while on the other she was distraught enough to need support while the noose was fastened around her neck. The lovers were hanged on either end of the same rope, and one broadsheet makes reference to Jeffryes expiring with her 'head in Swan's bosom' because of the way the rope twisted.

After her execution, and after the body had been left to hang for the requisite time, it is likely that the coffin was despatched to the family plot in Shropshire, as her parents were still living there. There is no record of their reaction to what had happened to their daughter as a result of their well-meant plans for her as a child. Interestingly, it seems that Elizabeth was in fact literate, as a number of letters she wrote to the similarly-circumstanced Mary Blandy (in prison for poisoning her father) were published after her death. Obviously, she had received a better level of education than if she'd stayed at home in Shropshire with her boat-builder father and the rest of her family. It seems that greed, pure and simple, was her downfall.

Child Murderers

Eighteenth & Nineteenth Centuries

This deals with five Essex women who were briefly infamous as a result of their crimes. The situation they found themselves in was not unusual in the eighteenth and nineteenth centuries, and nor was the decision they made. Giving birth to an unwanted child, especially if it was illegitimate, was no cause for celebration – just an extra mouth to feed in an age before any kind of benefits were payable for baby or mother, with the added burden of illegitimacy, a stigma that is now difficult to understand. Given the high rates of child mortality, these murders may well have been completely superfluous.

An early case was that of Elizabeth Butchill, born in about 1758 in Saffron Walden. At twenty-one she moved from the area, which was not able to provide her with enough work to maintain herself. Her chambermaid aunt and brewer uncle in

Saffron Walden. (Author's Collection)

Cambridge took her in so that she, too, could work alongside her aunt as a bed-maker at Trinity College. In the early hours of the morning of 6 January 1780, her aunt heard groans of distress. She heated peppermint water for her niece and provided her with hot flannels to relieve an apparent colic.

Just hours later, the body of a newborn female baby was found in the river near the college. A surgeon, Mr Bond, examined the body, and established that the skull had been fractured in several places. He was convinced that the child had been born alive and received its death by the wounds to its head. Her uncle had his suspicions, resulting in Elizabeth confessing that the child was hers and that she had thrown the child into the river and buried the placenta nearby.

Although it was more usual at the time for such desperate souls to be charged with concealment of the birth (a capital offence), in Elizabeth's case she was charged with murder, tried and convicted. Although she pleaded for mercy, the judge told her that since she had 'been deaf to the cries of the innocent' she, in her turn, would be shown no mercy in this world. A worthy clergyman visited her daily and administered the sacrament but Elizabeth, a young woman of previous good character, acknowledged the justice of the sentence and behaved in a modest, penitent manner.

Before her execution, she joined with the minister in prayer and sang the lamentation of a sinner. In March 1780 Elizabeth Butchill was launched into eternity watched by thousands of commiserating spectators who shed tears of pity for the unhappy girl.

* * *

Slightly more unusual was the later case of Elizabeth Langham, in that she was a married woman. She was the wife of a soldier in the 18th Light Dragoons stationed at Colchester. Mrs Langham was put on trial for the murder of her infant child. In defence, she pleaded that she did not intend to kill the child but was only trying to stop it from crying as she did not want her husband disturbed: he suffered some ridicule from comrades who were suspicious that the child was not his on account of its being born so soon after their marriage. Since her attempts to silence the child included tying a cord around its neck, there appears to have been some suspicion of her integrity and no benefit of doubt was accorded. Her sentence was, indicative of the period, the death penalty.

The time she spent in prison between sentence and execution seemed to have a dramatic effect on Elizabeth, who appeared physically and mentally wrecked by the experience. In front of a large crowd on Monday 19 March 1804, she had to be assisted on to the scaffold at Moulsham (Chelmsford) for her execution.

A soldier of the Light Dragoons. (Author's Collection)

Southminster. (Author's Collection)

Moving on forty years, yet another Elizabeth, Elizabeth Dean, gave birth in June at her widowed mother's cottage in Southminster. According to the local nurse, this confinement was a difficult one for Elizabeth, both before and after the birth. The baby boy was baptised Stephen James Belsham Dean at St Leonard's, the parents recorded as Stephen, a shoemaker, and Elizabeth, from Moulsham.

When baby Stephen was nineteen days old, Elizabeth left her mother's house aboard a mail cart heading for Chelmsford, needing to find a wet nurse as a result of her lack of milk and to track down her husband. Elizabeth broke her journey at the Saracen's Head in Runsell Green, and the landlady there remembered her feeding the baby but only with biscuits. At the end of a twelve-hour journey she arrived at the Beehive public house in Baddow Road, but her husband did not turn up.

An hour later, she was seen at the King's Head on Chelmsford High Street without the baby. A servant girl at the inn, Sarah Digby, noticed the wet and muddy state of Elizabeth's stockings and the gravel sticking to the soles of her boots before their owner went to her room.

The next morning, Elizabeth wrote a one-sentence letter to her husband, dating it two days earlier, and heading it Latchingdon, a distant village. She posted this brief missive on the way to visit her friend Sarah in nearby Writtle: 'I write to say that the poor child is no more, it dide (*sic*) last night.'

About this time, Oliver Turner had spotted something white in the water under the old footbridge next to Springfield Mill. Suspecting a body, Turner called at the mill to get help from the waggoner, Joseph White. The latter waded in and retrieved what was indeed a body – a baby in white muslin gown and cap. The baby was handed in to PC James Wright and just two days later, twenty-eight-year-old Elizabeth was arrested at her friend's house.

These events were recounted at Elizabeth's subsequent trial, reported in the *Chelmsford Chronicle*. Her plea of 'not guilty' to the charge of wilful murder had been given in a firm tone of voice.

The doctor who had examined the baby's body gave evidence that the boy had died from suffocation by drowning and had not been in the water for very long. The baby had no other signs of injury and was otherwise healthy.

The evidence against Elizabeth was obviously circumstantial – the baby's outfit identified by his grandmother, the wet stockings, the gravel on her boots which could have been from the river path. While the coroner had certainly felt that there was a case of wilful murder for her to answer, Elizabeth's solicitor gave an account of a woman weakened by lack of food and water, who may have been confused and unaware of her actions, or who may even have lost her grip on the child. Ryland, the solicitor, even tried to suggest that the baby was perhaps not young Stephen at all.

In this case, Elizabeth Dean (assuming she was married, for which there is no real evidence) was saved from the gallows by the behaviour of Stephen Dean. There were witnesses to his celebrations on receipt of Elizabeth's letter with a 'threepenny shot' of brandy with a drinking friend. Ryland further discredited Dean by quoting his insulting suggestions that the baby was a bastard, and with accusations that he had turned his pregnant wife out of doors.

His accounts of Elizabeth's suffering and his assassination of Stephen's character attracted large crowds into the court room at Shire Hall, Chelmsford. The jury's verdict of not guilty was greeted with approval from the citizens present.

✳ ✳ ✳

Shire Hall, Chelmsford. (Author's Collection)

Rebecca Law, aged twenty-four from Clavering, was less lucky nearly twenty years later. Her actions – the murder not only of her youngest child but also of her husband – were motivated to some extent by religious mania. When she in her turn appeared at Shire Hall, her plea was also not guilty.

Her husband, Samuel, a rat catcher, had spent a month in prison at Christmas for breaking a gate. Upon his release, he had collected his weak and hungry wife and youngest children from the workhouse at Saffron Walden, where they had spent Christmas. The Laws, who had been married seven years, had then spent most of the following Sunday at her mother's house where Samuel read the Bible, returning to their cottage at the end of the day.

Rebecca was back at her mother's house in Langley village soon after midnight, hammering at the door, crying out that her husband had been cut to pieces. She was in a distressed state, covered in blood, holding her six-year-old son by the hand.

One of the first men on the scene back at Starlings Green, the Laws' home, described the blood on the downstairs floor as coming from the upstairs bedroom. This was where he found Samuel Law's body spread-eagled on the floor, having succumbed to dozens of cuts about his head and shoulders; and the youngest child (a sixteen-week old baby) also dead in the corner. Shortly afterwards, a constable from Newport arrived at the scene with Rebecca, who admitted that she 'had chopped him with the chopper' – the weapon being found at the scene. She suggested at this stage that Samuel had mistreated her and threatened to kill her, though this did not explain why she had intended to murder any of her children.

The defending solicitor gave an account of Rebecca's weak state following the birth of her youngest child, so much so that she had needed a fly (a one-horse carriage) to transport her even as far as the workhouse. While there, she had lost a lot of blood as a result of some unnamed disorder, weakening her even further.

Samuel's Bible-readings on their last day together seemed to have been the final straw for Rebecca. The references had been to Christ being tempted by the devil, and Rebecca admitted that she had often been tempted to cut her own throat or her

Starlings Green, Clavering. (Author's Collection)

husband's. This timely reminder, therefore, resulted in her taking a chopper to where Samuel lay asleep, hitting him as hard as she could while he struggled. In her statement, she said that all the time she was hitting him she could hear the devils blundering up the stairs but she 'wasn't afraid'. He had treated her 'worse than a dog' and she had had a vision of the act that had taken place: she had known it was going to happen.

The workhouse surgeon gave evidence at her trial that she had been incoherent with symptoms of insanity, and the chaplain of the gaol referred to Rebecca's 'melancholy' and concerns as to whether she could be 'saved'. At this point, the Lord Chief Justice saw fit to explain to the jury that they had to decide if the prisoner was in such a state of mind at the time as to know that what she did was a crime. If not, they should acquit her on that ground, which the jury accordingly did. Rebecca, supported in the dock by the matron and the gaoler as she could hardly stand, seemed unaware of her lucky escape and was assisted from the court, to be retained indefinitely in an asylum.

※ ※ ※

One last interesting case – although there were many others – is that of Emily Pask, aged thirty-three in 1897. Emily was single, living with her father, a shepherd, and her two children, a girl of seventeen and a boy of thirteen, in a cottage in Little Walden Park, Saffron Walden. The four of them slept in just one room.

In June of that year, a small child was found dead in the washhouse attached to the cottage. The local doctor was called and gave evidence that the baby had probably been born alive but had died from strangulation. This meant that Emily – and her father – were both charged with wilful murder.

A crying baby – cause for murder? (Author's Collection)

The inquest revealed that Emily had a child in 1881 when living in Little Wratting, Suffolk: a child that had died at just one month old. Another child was the subject of an inquest in 1893, and this time the verdict was death by natural causes. Not surprisingly, the verdict was one of wilful murder at this stage.

Interestingly, at the subsequent Essex Assizes in Chelmsford, the judge told the jury that the question as to who was the father of the child could not be asked at this stage. Was this a hint at incest by any chance? There then followed a suggestion that the child might have turned over and suffocated accidentally, and the couple now decided to plead guilty to an alternative charge of concealment. As a result, they received a sentence of twelve months' imprisonment.

Imprisonment for such women, incidentally, was then very different to imprisonment now. An account in the *Essex Weekly News* in 1891, for instance, refers to hard mattresses stuffed with rope yarn laid on straight boards, meals of gruel and brown bread made from barley meal, with potatoes twice a week and soup twice a week. Days were spent picking strands of oakum (rope) apart or washing clothes until around 5.30 p.m. when the evening was free – for reading the Bible (the only reading material) or for thinking. Sundays meant less work but more time in the chapel, and the prison garb was a standard brown dress with brown bodice and white cap.

With hindsight, such cases, and such sentences, raise a lot of unanswered questions. The fame of these tortured women was short-lived; such fame was replicated by many on the lower rungs of 'civilised' society – not only in Essex of course.

Mary Wollstonecraft

1759–97

Although Mary Wollstonecraft's links with Essex were brief, someone with her reputation could hardly be left out. There are many biographies of this founder of feminism, the author of *Vindication of the Rights of Woman*, which detail her demands for male and female equality in every area including education and sexual behaviour. She was infamous, too, for her lifestyle. There was her relationship with the bisexual painter Henry Fuseli, her illegitimate daughter by writer Gilbert Imlay in Paris followed by her attempted suicide after their relationship broke up, and her pregnancy by philosopher William Godwin. Although she married Godwin, this was in spite of her reservations at losing her 'legal existence' by doing so.

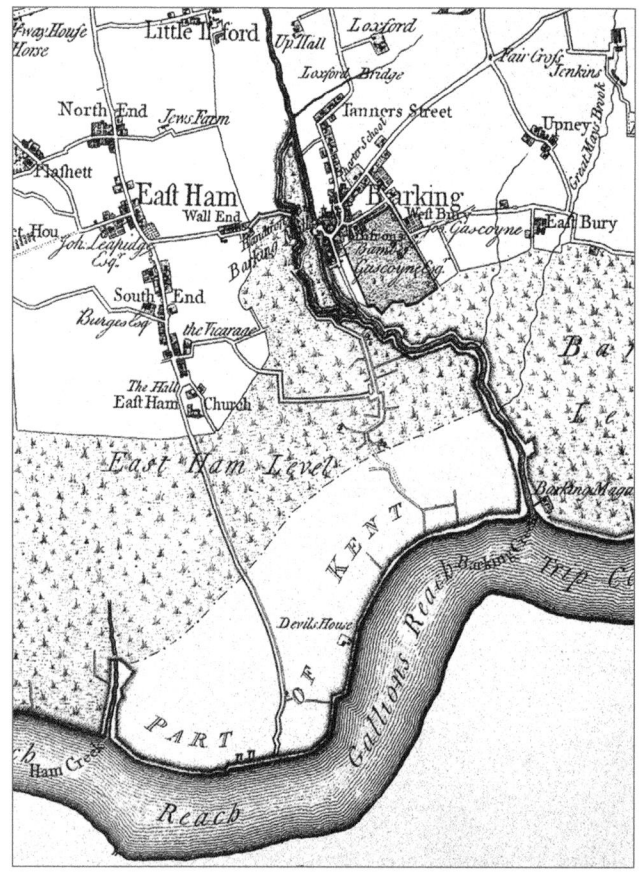

Chapman & Andre map of Barking, 1774. (Courtesy of www.foxearth.org.uk)

This paragon of infamy was born in Spitalfields, London. Her father, Edward, starting out in the family craft business as a handkerchief weaver, was not successful at hanging on to money. An even less-attractive trait was that when drunk or in a bad mood, he was not averse to beating any member of his family that was close at hand. Her Irish mother, Elizabeth, bore seven children, but only indulged and suckled Ned, her first born, who she knew would inherit the family wealth – if there was any left by the time he reached adulthood.

Edward didn't feel he was cut out for weaving, in spite of the promise of the Industrial Revolution, but wanted to better himself socially and live in the country. Although he knew nothing about crops or livestock, he decided to try his luck at farming, trying a number of different locations, mainly in Essex. These farms were mainly funded by the money he had inherited from his own father.

The first venture was at Epping in 1763, close to a former habitation of her father's. This farm was a little way off the Chelmsford road, near to the forest which covered a much larger area then than now. From there, the family moved to Barking in 1765, regarded as another move upwards, where they lived for three years. Mary relished the open-air situations of her early childhood, and was healthy and robust. She preferred outdoor activities to such contemptible attractions as dolls. In later years, she revisited the Barking area, renewing her acquaintance with the market and the crowded wharf.

Mary Wollstonecraft. (Author's Collection)

Things went badly for the family as their capital dwindled, and they set off for a farm near Beverley in Yorkshire, where the locals spoke in an accent she could barely understand and where the land was flat and undrained, flooding and freezing for miles in the winters.

When the family finally gave up on farming and returned to London in 1774, Mary was fifteen. She had hungrily acquired what education she could along the way, her only formal schooling being a few years at day school in Beverley. But it was enough for her to be able to acquire a level of independence, firstly as a governess and then as a writer, the latter not an easy way to make a living.

This famous feminist, philosopher and writer, brief resident of Essex, was reviled during her lifetime. She was described as a prostitute, an unsexed female and a hyena in petticoats. Time has changed such viewpoints dramatically.

Mary died a few months after her reluctant marriage, following the birth of her second daughter (of 'childbed fever' – probably septicemia following an abortive attempt to remove the placenta). It was this daughter, Mary, who went on to marry Percy Bysshe Shelley and write *Frankenstein*, following in her mother's literary footsteps. Essex should remember.

Anne Broadrick

Eighteenth Century

Probably not an Essex girl, but the notoriety of her Essex crime at the time meant that she merits inclusion. Her origins are obscured by time, but it seems likely that she was from South London, although there has been speculation that she was originally from the Grays area. How she met George Errington, wealthy London barrister and prominent Grays landowner, is also difficult to establish, but meet him she did. Anne became his mistress for some seven years, and would have spent quite a bit of time, therefore, in and around Grays, where he owned ninety acres.

George Errington, aged thirty-nine, was divorced from his wife around the time he met Anne, who was easily persuaded to move in with him. However, he did not marry her, but instead proposed to another 'available' local lady, seemingly younger and, by all accounts, an heiress who was higher up the social strata. To be fair, he did make provision for Anne's future when he turned her out in 1794, but Anne felt betrayed and aggrieved. She wrote him a letter in April of that year describing how wretched and miserable she was feeling, and pleading with him for one more meeting.

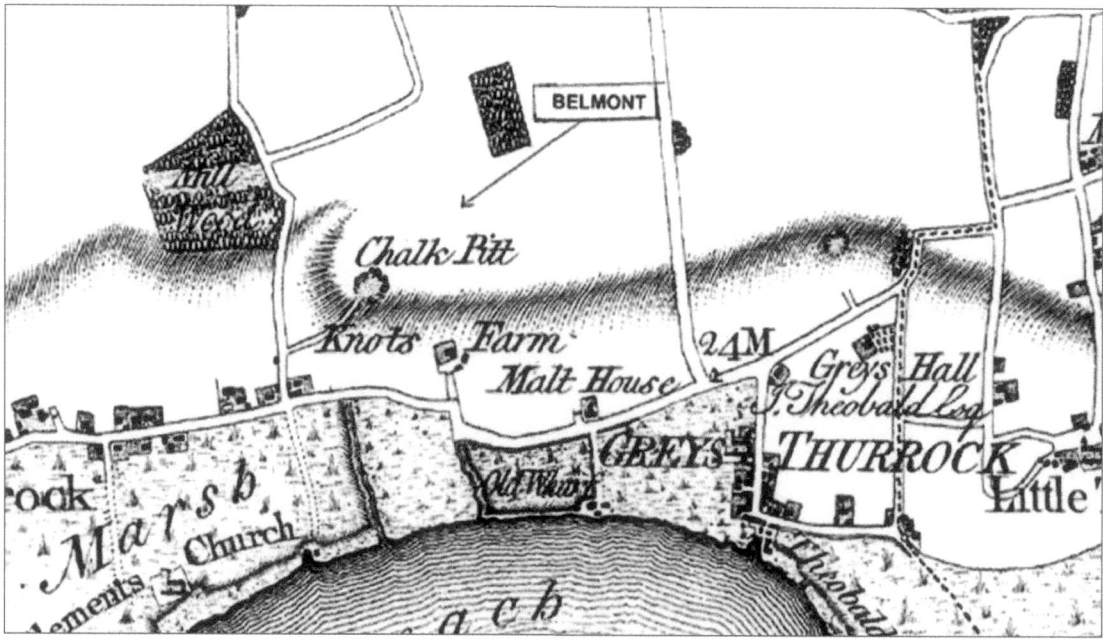

A map of the Grays area in the eighteenth century. (Courtesy of Thurrock Local History Society)

Early letter from Anne Broadrick to George Errington. (Courtesy of Tom Errington)

The first few lines of the original letter.

Friday morning Twelve o'clock
July 24th 1794

My Dear George,
As I am perfectly recovered from my late indisspossion you need not be afraid of coming to the house, for I am perfectly reconciled to my situvotion since my recovery. I recollect it is twelve months since you had the trouble of seeking out this mancion for me to live in by myself, yes George I do thank you for all the trouble you have had on my account as I have followed your last advice I donot need heney mor at present but this I have to bag of you that you will favour me with a visit . . . . .
This I must declare wether I ever see you again or not that know man as known me since you nor for meney years before and whot is mour I do not intend none ever shall as your liberality will ever I trust protect me from being oblidg to take up with heney one I have an advarsion to . . . . .
I rightly judged then that he (a 'friend' referred to earlier in the letter) had some one he wanted to get in my place but I fear there is some yet more that I canot possibly surjist that keep you from me if the power of licencious tongues can keep us apart I am sur we never shall meet again . . . . .
I can most sollomly declare my constancy to you. You always declare how much you loved me in prefference to heney woman you ever knew, have heney thing to say to me now come and commune with your own mouth, as your company will me mor pleasure then the best Bank noat you can present me with.
Believe me yours sencearley.

There was a reference in this letter to the terrible revenge that could be the result of the 'rage and vengeance of a disappointed woman', because she threatened that, if he did not accede to her request, she would seek him out in 'the farthest corner of the globe' and replicate the actions of Charlotte Corday, who assassinated 'the monster Marat'. Even so, her request was refused, and Errington ignored a number of subsequent letters, although she warned him to prepare 'for the fatal alternative'.

Anne was as good as her word. On Friday morning, 15 May 1795, she dressed herself elegantly, intending to take the Southend coach (starting out at Whitechapel). She just missed the coach and had to resort to hiring a chaise and driver, instructing him to overtake the coach, which he did after nine miles, enabling her to change vehicles. The coach passed close to Errington's property and he – and his new wife of eight months, Eleanor – saw her approaching on foot along the drive to their home. Errington suggested his wife make herself scarce so that he could deal with the persistent Anne, but Mrs Errington said she would deal with Anne herself.

Anne was not so easily deterred. She knew the layout of the house well, and rushed past Eleanor to search for her quarry, finding him in the drawing room. Once he was in her sights, literally, Anne took a small brass-barrelled pistol from her pocket and announced, 'I am come to perform my dreadful promise', before firing point blank at his heart. Eleanor, behind her, fainted, but Mr Errington stayed unexpectedly upright. This turn of events alarmed Anne to such an extent that she threw the pistol on the carpet towards the servants who had arrived in response to the sound of the commotion.

At least one surgeon (accounts differ), soon attended, but the nature of the wound – the ball had cut through three ribs and lodged in Errington's back under the shoulder blade – made it impossible for him to do more than dress the wound. A local magistrate, Zachariah Button, arrived on the scene to question Anne, who made no attempt to leave. Although Errington entreated that she should not be detained, she was despatched to Chelmsford gaol. While in prison, she managed to remain composed for a few days until Errington's death was reported, at which point she broke down, lamenting her actions. The inquest was short and sweet with a verdict of 'Wilful murder by the hands of Anne Broadrick'.

The trial, at Chelmsford Shire Hall in July, took up a lot of space in the nationals as well as the local press. Anne was accompanied in court by three female friends and her apothecary. There was, it has to be said, an underlying element of sympathy for Anne in that much was made of Errington's rather messy divorce, of the fact that he had married his first wife when she was already pregnant, a wife who had subsequently been found guilty of multiple adultery. Reference was also made to his other 'female attachments'. Anne, incidentally, was presented as something of a victim at her trial, having been deserted by the previous man in her life who had 'gone to India under some circumstances of pecuniary distress'. It was not unusual for attractive women of the period to secure a reasonable standard of living by being an acknowledged 'kept' mistress, an acceptable social status although not quite the fount of respectability. Anne fitted the bill, being described as 'possessed of considerable accomplishments'

Historic Grays. (Author's Collection)

with a 'fine figure' and 'personal charms', although dressed in mourning for her trial 'without powder'. Another newspaper described her as 'elegant' and 'engaging' with 'light blue eyes' and 'light brown hair', with a maximum age of thirty years.

The prosecution (conducted by Mr Garrow) reminded the jury that they must be perfectly satisfied that the prisoner was in possession of her reasoning faculties, otherwise it was insanity and not 'the moral agent' which perpetuated the 'bloody act'. George Errington's servant gave evidence of Anne's arrival, of hearing the pistol shot and his master crying out 'Oh God, I am shot'. When he went to his master's aid, he described him as 'all over blood' and then rode a mile to get the nearest surgeon, together with two constables. It seems at this point that Anne was suspected of having a second pistol which she intended to use on herself, but was not given the opportunity of doing so.

Mr Shepherd acted for Anne at the trial. He called on William Bush, the driver of the whiskey (a light two-wheeled chaise that 'whisked along'), to give an account of the journey, and of Anne's behaviour. Bush recalled stopping to pay four pence for the turnpike en route, and remembered Anne complaining firstly that he drove too fast and then that he drove too slowly. He summed her up as a 'crazy woman'. John Eves, a Grays butcher who needed to visit Smithfield regularly, also gave evidence of attempting to deliver letters from Anne to Errington which the latter told him to return – one was produced in court, suggesting a meeting between the two at the Dog and Partridge, Stifford.

Later letter from Anne Broadrick to George Errington. (Courtesy of Tom Errington)

Further witnesses were quoted in the press. A baker who had supplied Anne with bread told how she often gave him as much as a half crown for a threepenny loaf but shut the door without accepting the change, obviously interpreted as a sign of madness rather than of generosity. Anne's brother-in-law gave evidence that her mother had been deemed insane, as was a sister. Her ex-charwoman also talked about Anne's 'oddness' and how she had been known to throw boiling water at her if the doorsteps were not cleaned satisfactorily. Similarly, other servants told stories of her ringing bells at night for attention, and of her propensity for carrying a pistol to threaten 'lax' employees. Such staff were employed, incidentally, at Anne's South London home which was funded by Errington.

Apparently, the jury took just a couple of minutes to reach a verdict of not guilty. Those in court applauded the verdict. Anne was averse to suggestions of lunacy to excuse her crime but had been offered no real alternative that offered her freedom. She was therefore ordered to be detained as a 'lunatic' and, in the October issue of *The Times* was reported to be in the workhouse of Lambeth Parish. This must have been a devastating blow to one used to a very different lifestyle. But no doubt preferable to the alternative.

Postscript: Some of Anne's original letters are now in the possession of Mr Tom Errington, a descendant of the unfortunate victim, who still lives locally. Parts of these are reproduced with his permission – note the interesting spelling. Just as worthy of note is the deterioration between the style of Anne's approach in July 1794 and that of 1795 (this latter being one of those produced in court), when she has moved from 'My dear George' to 'Dear Sir'.

Mary Anne Clarke

1776–1852

Here we have that classic example of an ambitious actress who found it more profitable to be the mistress of an influential royal. From lowly origins in London, she was entertaining the glitterati of London by 1805 with the help of twenty servants and three cooks, drinking from wine glasses costing a remarkable two guineas each.

Daphne du Maurier, apparently a great-great-granddaughter of Mary Anne, wrote a book of the same name fictionalising her ancestor's life story. Her own research confirmed many links with Essex. She gives some detail regarding Mary Anne's education at a young ladies' boarding school in Ham (now East and West Ham) until the age of fifteen-and-a-half. By that time Mary Anne had acquired all the necessary accoutrements of refinement, writing a 'fair hand', sewing and embroidery, with proficiency in reading, history, drawing, English literature – and at playing the harp.

According to Du Maurier, this level of education was paid for by the overseer of the printing works that employed her father, which does seem the most likely explanation. Mary Anne had declined his offer of a position as housekeeper, a job title that concealed a multitude of potentially degrading duties. She favoured a union with the young, attractive Joseph Clarke, whom she had apparently met when he was a lodger at her family home in the heart of unsavoury central London. At the time of their marriage, Mary Anne, not yet eighteen, was establishing herself as an actress, playing roles at such popular venues as the Haymarket Theatre in London's West End. But Joseph, the proprietor of a stone masonry business, seemed to offer the cultured and rich antecedents Mary Anne craved.

Things did not go according to plan, however. After they had three children together (a son and two daughters) Joseph got into financial difficulties, and she left him, with her subsequent liaisons culminating in a relationship with Frederick Augustus Hanover, Duke of York, from 1803, a probable member of Mary Anne's smitten audience. It seems that Joseph reappeared in her life not long after, threatening the Duke of York with proceedings for adultery. It is quite likely that Joseph's threatening letters drove the duke into the arms of the next mistress waiting in the wings. As George III's second son and Commander-in-Chief of the Army (he was the Grand Old Duke of York in history), Frederick had reason to be worried.

One of Mary Anne's admirers, when HRH was cooling, was William Coxhead-Marsh of Essex, 'stiff with property' whose generosity she could probably count on to loan her a house at Loughton. It was then an area used as a retreat for artists,

Colchester Barracks. (Author's Collection)

intellectuals and wealthy merchants from London. Lolling about at Loughton, however, yawning at tales of woodcock, partridge and pigeon and trying to enjoy autumn in Essex, could not destroy the memories of London power and status.

At one period she had her mother to stay with her in Loughton, around the same time that her brother was asked to leave his Colchester regiment. Mary Anne felt it was important to see that all her family were settled. She hired a lawyer to deal with brother Charley's pending court martial at Colchester, managing to clear him of one charge (of a fraud against the paymaster, involving the presentation of worthless bills) but not of the other (absenting himself without leave). The court case figured largely in the newspapers of 1808, as did the news of Charley's sentence: to be cashiered. Coxhead-Marsh became uncomfortable with the media references to Loughton Lodge, and appears to have withdrawn his protection.

It seems that Mary Anne had been promised £1,000 a year by the duke in addition to the elegant London home and all its trappings, but this allowance was not paid as regularly as it should have been and Mary Anne found a way of boosting her income. There were always those seeking promotion – military, civil, even clerical – and Mary Anne was happy to take money from them in return for her influence. Her affair with the duke turned into a political scandal in 1809 when he was charged with corruption as a result of her activities. The principal witness for the prosecution was listed as: 'Mary Anne Clarke of Loughton Lodge in the County of Essex, a widow' (although it is not clear whether in fact Joseph was dead). In spite of the way the duke had shaken her off, exposed her to poverty and infamy, and refused her a promised annuity, all damning in

Cartoon of Mary Anne Clarke. (Courtesy of cartoonstock.com)

the eyes of his public persona, the duke was acquitted on the charges of corruption. The scandal was the Watergate of Regency London with major coverage in every newspaper.

His ex-mistress's subsequent threat to publish her memoirs – to pay for her children's future – resulted in the duke's resignation as Commander-in-Chief of the Army and in a legal agreement being drawn up between Mary Anne and her former lover. He agreed that she would receive £10,000, an annuity for life of £400, and £200 for each of her daughters. Blackmail? Some would say so. Adept political manoeuvring would be another interpretation.

This is not a story with a happy ending. Mary Anne could not lay down her pen, and libellous publications continued, resulting in her spending nine months in Marshalsea prison. The only bright spark during this period was the commissioning of her son, George, to the 17th Light Dragoons, thanks to a promise made long ago by HRH which she had not expected to materialise.

York Hill, Loughton. (Author's Collection)

There was to be no more time spent in Essex for Mary Anne and her daughters; not even in England, where, after her release, she was *persona non grata*. She lived in France for a number of years, in constrained circumstances, and died alone in Boulogne in 1852, her death reported in *The Times* by the Paris correspondent. Had she been born two hundred years later, she would have been in demand by the likes of Richard and Judy or *Hello* magazine. Back in Essex, incidentally, it is quite likely that York Hill and York House in Loughton are named as a result of the connection with the Duke of York. As for Loughton Lodge, it is unrecognisable now as two separate dwellings.

Postscript: Anyone interested in reading Mary Anne's memoirs should hunt out one of the following, both with the pithy titles popular at the time:

The Authentic and Impartial Life of Mrs Mary Anne Clarke, Including Numerous Royal and Other Original Letters, and Anecdotes of Distinguished Persons, Which Have Escaped Suppression, with a Compendious View of the Whole Proceedings, Illustrative of the Late Important Investigation of the Conduct of His Royal Highness the Duke of York, &C. &C. and a Curious Poem, T. Kelly, London, 1809.

The Rival Princes; Or, A Faithful Narrative of Facts, Relating to Mrs M.A. Clarke's Political Acquaintance with Colonel Wardle, Major Dodd, &C. &C. &C., Who Were Concerned in the Charges against the Duke of York; Together with a Variety of Authentic and Important Letters, and Curious and Interesting Anecdotes of Several Persons of Political Notoriety, Printed for the author, and published by C. Chapple, London, 1810.

Lady Smugglers

Nineteenth Century

These ladies have proved elusive, but they did exist, in Essex as elsewhere. For obvious reasons, they kept a low profile, but some of their stories have survived. For instance, in the 1840s, Mrs Gregson kept a chandler's shop and tobacconists in the churchyard of St Margaret's at Barking, not far from the creek. It seems she 'employed' a number of young lads, all under sixteen, rendering them immune from prosecution. These lads, known as Mother Gregson's Gang, were paid 4*d* for every pound of tobacco they brought her, mainly retrieved from fishing boat crews who were smuggling it in. Barking then had, perhaps surprisingly, the largest fishing fleet in the country, with 200 smacks owned by one family alone.

Mrs Gregson supplied large tobacconists and City merchants with her smuggled goods. On at least one occasion, she was able to produce official receipts for duty paid to customs officers when her premises were searched – her contacts in London came in

St Margaret's, Barking. (Author's Collection)

River Colne, Colchester. (Author's Collection)

Rowhedge. (Author's Collection)

useful. But she was not always able to pull in favours, for there are records of her being fined at least twice for having 'uncustomed tobacco' in her shop. Further north, the River Colne en route to Colchester Hythe Port was ideally placed for smuggling. One young captain, John Pim, would navigate his cutter on a moonless night, looking out for the signal from his lover, Miss Molly. She was described as a lovely young woman with clear blue eyes like cornflowers and flowing golden hair like buttercups: a veritable garden of beauty.

Leigh-on-Sea. (Author's Collection)

If the coast was clear, with no signs of customs men, Molly would lift the blind in a front window of the attractive Georgian house where she lived with her mother. Molly's fat cat, The Bosun, would sit alongside the lighted candle she placed on the window-sill, and Molly would receive a kiss for her efforts from the captain after his contraband had been unloaded.

It seems that even after the couple were married, living in the same house – called the Darkhouse, on the corner of Darkhouse Lane at Rowhedge – they continued to indulge in a spot of smuggling to boost their income.

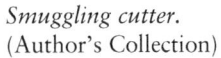

Smuggling cutter. (Author's Collection)

The most successful petticoated smuggler seems to have been Elizabeth Little of Leigh-on-Sea. She had a shop where the Peter Boat car park is now, selling all kinds of goods, much of it seemingly contraband. Her speciality was in luxury fabrics such as lace and silks, which were subject to heavy taxation at the time. She was educated and intellectual and well able to handle a boat. In fact, Elizabeth and her brothers visited France on a regular basis for their booty, picking up French wines for Elizabeth's dinner parties en route.

Of course, the coastguards at Leigh in the mid-nineteenth century were always trying to trap their suspect. The nearest they came was when they tried to follow the Littles into Barking Creek, unsuccessfully because of the shallow waters. Elizabeth removed her contraband into a hearse she hired from a nearby undertaker, hiding one wounded brother inside while she disguised herself as a black-clad mourner – and got away with it yet again.

Most lady smugglers were unlikely, however, to be particularly ladylike, and would often have been indistinguishable among their male counterparts. Their identities and their stories were concealed from public scrutiny, sadly for modern historians.

Mary May

1810–48

Nothing too exciting happened in the little village of Wix until 1848. Harwich was the nearest town in this part of north-east Essex, and villagers on the whole struggled to eke out their existence. Mary May and her second husband, Robert, managed to maintain an income from selling bread and foodstuffs. They also had to provide for their two-year-old son and for Mary's ten-year-old son from her first marriage, William Everett. To assist their finances, they had two lodgers: William Constable, Mary's half-brother (known as Spratty Watts for some now inexplicable reason), and James Simpson.

Spratty worked as a pedlar or a farm hand and was working in a field near home when struck down by pain and vomiting on Thursday 8 June. Dr William Thompson from Manningtree called to see him on Saturday, and prescribed some medicine, but Spratty did not recover. He died on Sunday and was buried with no fuss or enquiry – as was common. However, when Mary claimed her allotted £10 for funeral expenses from the Harwich 'Death Club' (an insurance scheme for the poor), an efficient clerk spotted that Mary had lied about her own and her brother's ages (as they were over

Wix. (Author's Collection)

Harwich. (Author's Collection)

the maximum accepted on the insurance). Not only that, but the insurance had only been effected shortly before Spratty's death. Alarm bells rang and Spratty's body was exhumed and, finally, medically examined.

A post-mortem was carried out by the original visiting doctor (William Thompson) on 30 June. He sent the stomach and its contents to Professor Taylor who revealed that he had found ten grains of arsenic in the stomach, three times the amount needed to kill a man. Given the motive of the insurance money (£10 would have covered a lot more than the funeral expenses and represented about six months' wages for the average working man) and the many opportunities she had of administering the arsenic, Mary May was arrested.

Her trial took place in July at Chelmsford Shire Hall. One of those who gave evidence was Mary's other lodger, James Simpson. He claims that Mary had told him about the Harwich Death Club and had said 'Please God . . . [she] should have ten pounds out . . . and get a donkey and cart'.

Evidence was also given of her attempting to buy arsenic (available over the counter, often used for killing rats), although none was actually found or produced in court. Her son, in spite of his age, was called upon to give evidence and told the court that he had seen his mother put 'a white powder' into Spratty's porter on several occasions.

The doctor and his assistant (who had made up the medicine) assured the court that there was nothing poisonous in what had been prescribed, again without any evidence being provided.

Mary's haste in applying for the funeral funds, following so soon after her joining the Death Club, seemed to have swayed the jury in spite of an impassioned speech from her defence counsel. They took just twenty minutes to find her guilty, at which point Mary declared her innocence, too late to make any difference to the judge who condemned her to death after emphasising the wickedness of her crime and urging her to make peace with her God in the short time remaining to her.

The newspapers at the time suggested that Mary may have committed other similar crimes – her first husband and earlier children had all died, after all. Her character was also tainted by reports of her offering sexual favours to the policeman guarding her in her condemned cell.

Even so, Mary resolutely refused to confess and instead pointed the finger in different directions. She seems to have accused James Simpson at one point, and has also been quoted as saying that Spratty was struck down by 'a policeman'. There certainly seemed to have been plenty of people who believed she was innocent. During the month between her trial and execution, a petition of 1,400 signatures was raised for a commutation of her sentence. This was all to no effect, however. It was, of course, another century before capital punishment was brought to an end.

Mary was executed in August 1848, on a scaffold erected above the entrance to the gaol. A crowd of well over 3,000 gathered, as was common for such an event, especially as the last execution in Chelmsford was nine years earlier, and it had been forty-four years since a woman had been executed there. Her last words were 'Good-bye; may the Lord have mercy on my soul'.

The Victorian approach to arsenic. (Author's Collection)

Interestingly, though not unusually, this murder trial resulted in a ballad, which may well have helped Mary's fame linger on. Here's a sample verse:

> In Essex boundary I did dwell,
> My brother lived with me,
> In a little village called Wix,
> Not far from Manningtree.
> In a burial club I entered him,
> On purpose him to slay:
> And to obtain the burial fees
> I took his life away.

It is, of course, quite likely that the ready availability of arsenic resulted in a lot of unsuspected murders, but some went just too far, as the following chapter will reveal.

Sarah Chesham

1809–51

It was to be only three years after Mary May's execution that another Essex woman followed her to the gallows. Sarah Parker was born in Clavering and married local lad Richard Chesham by the age of nineteen, giving birth to her first daughter seven months later. Richard often worked away from home as an agricultural labourer, but he must have come home quite often because the couple had a further five children during the next eleven years. The size of the family, failing crops at the time and the general lack of money meant that they survived on the poverty line.

In 1847, two of her sons, Joseph and James, died following violent stomach pains and sickness, initially attributed to cholera. Post-mortems were carried out on the boys, proving they had been poisoned, but not how or why. At the time Sarah was allegedly having an affair with a Clavering farmer, Thomas Newport, and she defended herself by

Clavering church. (Author's Collection)

Victorian policeman.
(Author's Collection, from an original *Punch*, 1899)

Newport, location of police station.
(Author's Collection)

accusing Thomas of instigating the deaths. She was brought to trial for the wilful murder of her two sons, but acquitted due to lack of evidence. There was no proof that arsenic had been administered, nor was any found in her possession. Thomas, who had been charged with aiding and abetting Sarah in administering poison, was released on bail.

Chelmsford gaol. (Author's Collection)

Sarah was also implicated at the time in the suspicious death of neighbour Lydia Taylor's baby. In this case, the trial was abandoned early on because there was no evidence of poison in the child's body, suggesting natural causes.

Just three years later, Sarah's husband died and was buried without much ceremony in Clavering church. Aged just forty-three, he had been suffering for some time from a lung disease with bouts of violent sickness. Local gossip, not unexpectedly, suggested that Sarah could have been up to her old tricks – the neighbours had never agreed with the jury and she became known as Sally Arsenic. A post-mortem revealed tiny amounts of arsenic in Richard's body, but there was not enough for a case against his widow, at least not until the police spoke to neighbour Hannah Phillips. Hannah gave an account of how Sarah had offered advice on what Hannah could do about her unhappy marriage, rather drastic advice, and Superintendent John Clarke from Newport police station got authorisation from the Home Secretary to remove a bag of rice from Sarah's home. The rice, when analysed at Guy's Hospital, was found to have been mixed with arsenic and Sarah was arrested.

Cartoon. (Author's Collection, from an original *Punch*, 1840)

When Sarah appeared at Chelmsford Assizes in March 1851, she, unsurprisingly, protested her innocence yet again. She blamed the arsenic in Richard's body on food

Imprisonment Victorian style.
(Author's Collection)

provided by others when she had been ill. It was Hannah Phillips' evidence that swayed the jury this time to come up with a verdict of guilty. She revealed the details of Sally Arsenic's advice: bake a pie of liver and lights (animal lungs) with a seasoning of Sarah's special poison and that would rid Hannah of her violent husband for good. Hannah also claimed that Sarah had admitted to poisoning baby Solomon Taylor. Sarah was convicted of administering poison with intent and sentenced to death at Springfield (Chelmsford).

The execution took place at the same time as that of another murderer who had strangled his mistress (Thomas Drory) and attracted even more people than usual – as many as ten thousand. It was quite a day out, by all accounts, with hawkers selling food and broadsheets, with plenty of women dressed in their best bonnets, accompanied by their children, and an air of festival complete with pickpockets. Sarah took a few more minutes than Drory to die, her lightweight body swinging on the end of the executioner's rope, and her coffin was then taken back to Clavering church on a cart driven by her oldest son, Philip.

Sally Arsenic had, unwittingly, led to a change in the law on selling poisons. Up to this point, it had been too readily available, offering a drastic but satisfactory way out for women with too many mouths to feed or with no-good husbands. Arsenic, subsequently, could only be sold to adult males and only if they gave details of their name, address and reason for purchase. Sadly, a lot of lives had been lost in the meantime.

Kitty O'Shea
(or Katharine Parnell)

1845–1921

Kitty was born Katharine Wood in Glazenwood in the parish of Bradwell. Her father was Sir John Page Wood, a former secretary to Queen Caroline, and her mother was an illustrator and romantic novelist. From 1882, Katharine's father spent a few years as vicar of Cressing, south of Bradwell and Braintree. She was the thirteenth child and unsurprisingly this was a crowded – and damp – place without the benefit of the beautiful gardens at Glazenwood.

Her earliest memories were, however, of Rivenhall Place, a substantial house the family rented from a friend soon after her birth. In her memoirs, she recalls being a delicate child who was kept out of doors as much as possible. She enjoyed feeding the

Cressing church. (Author's Collection)

Rivenhall Place. (Author's Collection)

swans on the lake and fetching the letters before breakfast from the post office half a mile away, delaying the latter process by visiting the Rivenhall curate whose letters she also collected. She also had the benefit of her own pony, although this seems to have been purchased in part to assist in strengthening her spine.

Winter months saw Katharine indoors making tea and toast for her father, and attempting to plot stories which her more competent mother and sister were able to adapt into full-blown novels, in many cases successfully. It does seem that the flickering shadows and large gloomy rooms of this dwelling also left her with some spooky memories. Her father also allowed her to accompany him when he was called upon as visiting magistrate to Chelmsford gaol, visits which made quite an impression.

Her childhood oozed culture and provided the sort of company (such as Anthony Trollope, who enjoyed the area's hunting) that made up for the lack of a formal education. She had the added advantage of learning astronomy at the hands of the replacement vicar of Cressing, and was taught to play the organ by the blind vicar of Witham. Once Katharine had acquired the necessary skills for a wife and mother in the landed gentry – which included housecraft, embroidery and music – she was ready to find a husband.

Further south was the country seat of her brother-in-law, Belhus at Aveley, and this seems to have been where Katharine first became attracted to William O'Shea, the son of an Irish solicitor. Her older brothers and sisters, seven of whom survived childhood, were for the most part either soldiers or married to soldiers, and she mixed in such circles. They had already met at Aldershot where her brother Frank was stationed. Katharine, now nineteen, therefore knew of William, a handsome young officer in the

Belhus. (Author's Collection)

18th Hussars, as a superb athlete and a first-class steeple-chase rider, and their meeting at Belhus consolidated her interest.

At the end of his visit, William presented Katharine with a poem, and, although he was not the first choice of her father, they often met at Belhus from then on, and Willie became a regular caller at Rivenhall over a three-year period. The year of her father's death (1866) was a sad one for Katharine, but it gave Willie the opportunity for his persistence to pay off and they married in Brighton in January 1867. After the wedding, they took off for Spain where William had taken a partnership in his uncle's bank. However, this proved unsuccessful and they returned to a stud farm in Hertfordshire to a life of entertaining and gambling. Katharine was able to be re-united with the pony from her Rivenhall childhood now they were back in England.

Willie's extravagances led to the necessity for him to sell his brood mares, and soon afterwards he was declared bankrupt. The couple came to rely on a wealthy aunt, who enabled them to settle in Brighton where their first child (a boy) was born, and who also found them a home in London where their next two children (daughters) came into the world. They did revisit Rivenhall on at least one occasion in 1869, when Katharine's eldest surviving brother, Frank, was dying of consumption.

Her husband's next bright idea, a shot at being MP for County Clare, led to her meeting Charles Stewart Parnell, the 'uncrowned' King of Ireland who was destined to bring Home Rule to his country. Their attraction was immediate, although she was a little older than he. She writes in her memoirs of his 'curiously burning eyes' and of her reaction to someone 'wonderful – and different'. They started meeting each other regularly, and his letters from 1880, whenever he was away on parliamentary business, were only ambiguous if you were unaware of their relationship, e.g. references to the 'difficulty of . . . living . . . in the absence of a certain kind and fair face.'

Parnell was imprisoned in Dublin for seven months in 1881–2, accused of masterminding the peasant agitation for land. His letters continued from gaol, now utilising invisible ink. While he was in prison, Katharine gave birth to his daughter, although the baby lived just a few months. Their relationship produced another two daughters in 1883 and 1884.

Parnell had no time for O'Shea's political ineptitude and preferred Katharine, based in London, as the intermediary between himself and Gladstone, the British (Liberal) Prime Minister. This seemed to have suited Gladstone as well as it suited Parnell. Gladstone felt that a combination of Liberal and Irish MPs would defeat Tory opposition to the Home Rule for Ireland Bill.

Kitty O'Shea.
(Courtesy of MultiText Project in History)

Captain O'Shea finally instituted divorce proceedings when Katharine's generous aunt (Mrs Wood) died. Any scandal prior to her death could have resulted in Katharine's disinheritance. In 1891, once the divorce decree was absolute, Parnell married Katharine. The wedding took place at a register office because vicars near their Brighton home would not marry them. There was too much prejudice then in existence against divorce, with Katharine labelled in the press as the adulterous seducer of a gallant leader.

Parnell's opponents in Ireland felt that 'Kitty O'Shea' (Kitty being a slang name for a prostitute) had a sinister influence on Parnell's decisions. Even Gladstone now abandoned the Irish/Liberal partnership. *The Times*, seemingly anti-Parnell at this time, felt that the marriage was indecently clandestine, and not a step towards respectability. In addition, Katharine's divorce was not accepted by Irish Catholics, and pressure was put on her Protestant husband to give up his leadership of the Irish Parliamentary Party. The opposition Parnell had been fighting in Ireland and the scandal of the O'Shea divorce case had such an impact on his fragile constitution that he died at their Brighton home only four months after their wedding, aged barely forty-five.

The proceeds from her aunt's estate were challenged and Katharine found herself struggling financially. She used the name O'Shea to publish a book about Parnell (subtitled *His Love Story and Political Life*) in 1914, which helped it to sell. Nevertheless, living in such grand establishments as Rivenhall Place was now a dim memory.

She died at a modest Littlehampton address one year before Ireland (i.e. Southern Ireland, or Eire) gained its independence – a country she may not have visited, but on whose history she made an indefinable impact.

Ellen Willmott

1858–1934

Warley Place and its 33 acres, near Brentwood, was purchased in 1875 by Ellen Willmott's father, a solicitor. The family had been living in Middlesex, but Ellen was looking forward to the move. One of her two sisters had died of diphtheria a few years earlier, and young Ellen and her remaining sister Rose were looking forward to a fresh start in, hopefully, healthier surroundings. They had inherited a love of gardening from their mother and Warley was going to offer far more scope.

It was Warley Place and its gardens that were going to put Ellen Willmott into Essex history. This slight redhead was described by those who knew her as ambitious, proud, intelligent, beautiful, with a complex personality by turns munificent and mean,

Warley Place. (Courtesy of Essex Record Office)

vain and implacable, headstrong and imperious. She remained single and eccentric, infamous for her obsessive love of gardening and landscaping. This is illustrated by the way she was said to have scrabbled through the trugs of weeds her gardeners pulled up, checking for stray seedlings – and woe betide the guilty gardener if one had been thrown out in error. Ellen really seemed to have preferred the company of flowers and shrubs to that of flesh and blood.

Her first achievement was the alpine garden she started at the age of twenty-one with a £1,000 birthday gift from her godmother – it took her three years before she was satisfied with the project. Warley Place gardens eventually incorporated a boating lake with landing stage and Swiss chalet, a group of heated glasshouses, walled garden, a herbaceous walk, park-like meadows, a unique collection of roses and 600 varieties of narcissus, with 100,000 plants in all. At her productive peak, Ellen employed 104 uniformed gardeners, although this probably included those maintaining properties she eventually owned in Switzerland, Holland, France and Italy.

She received an astonishing number of awards for exhibits at the Royal Horticultural Society's shows, including several medals for her achievements. Additionally, she wrote gardening books, published a book of photographs of professional standard, advised on garden design and planting and owned a lathe which she used to work with wood and ivory.

Her sister Rose had married in 1891 and moved away and Ellen had inherited considerable wealth by the 1890s following the death of her parents. But she knew how to spend, helping to finance expeditions to China and the Middle East to hunt for rare specimens. Her most famous book, *Genus Rosa*, confirmed her expertise on the subject of roses, but it cost her vast sums commissioning paintings for the illustrations.

Closer to home, she was building on a reputation for unusual behaviour. For instance, it was not unusual for Ellen to walk home from Brentwood station after an evening in London – a mile and a half – rather than call for driver and transport, regardless of the weather or her mode of dress. This was a long, unlit walk until reaching the gas-lit lamps on the main gates of Warley Place, which kept burning all night. She did, however, have to ring to gain entrance, the doors being bolted on the inside by now, disturbing one of the youngest gardeners who would leave his bed to admit her. Such gardeners, incidentally, were aware that they would be fired if they allowed a single weed to thrive.

By the 1920s, Ellen had been forced to dispense with her coachman, groom, stable-boy, lady's maid, footman, chauffeur, cook, parlourmaid and housemaid. Only a handful of gardeners remained. A new housekeeper who arrived in 1924 (to replace one accused of stealing) revealed that there was an enormous disparity between the grandeur of the furnishings and the standard of cleanliness. Although the structure of the house included sixteen bedrooms, a chapel, a music room and a library, Ellen's efforts were still concentrated on her beloved gardens.

On trips to London, she wore buttonholes of impossibly obscure flowers, hoping that fellow members of the Royal Horticultural Society would be unable to identify them. An incident is recorded with regard to Ellen forgetting her gloves on a visit to see Queen Mary in London and having to borrow a shabby pair from a friend at the station, prompting the housekeeper (Annie Cotterell) to take on some of the lady's maid duties, ensuring that her employer left the house suitably garbed.

Another visit to London (1928) when dressed below par meant that she was actually arrested for shoplifting in Galeries Lafayette in Regent Street. She had dropped her receipt – for a scarf – between the till and the exit, and the store detective took what he considered to be appropriate action. When the manager heard Ellen on the telephone to Queen Mary, however, followed by the prompt arrival of the king's private secretary, he offered her immediate compensation for the mistake. Declining, Ellen Willmott, instead of being publicly cleared of shoplifting, found herself spending a night in Marlborough Street police station, being brought up before the magistrates the following morning. Thanks to her high-profile defence, and witnesses that included the Chief Constable of Essex, she was acquitted, but took the opportunity to proclaim the unfairness of a system that would have certainly seen her convicted had she been an inarticulate woman with less high-profile acquaintances. Was she drawing attention to the unjust treatment of women prevailing at the time, or was she drawing attention to her own predicament? Whatever the reason, she decided to highlight the injustice by claiming damages from the store for false imprisonment and malicious prosecution, but, a year later, *The Times* reported that the civil action had been honourably settled.

There would seem to have been other occasions when Ellen appeared in court – mainly for non-payment of rates – but this has also been described by her contemporaries as a way of avoiding jury service. It was during this period that Ellen felt obliged to close her bank account at Brentwood, and to start selling off some of her books (1,400 of them) and her jewellery. Money to pay her housekeeper, her long-suffering butler, and her remaining gardeners was often difficult to come by. By now she was almost used to being in debt, and there is evidence that as early as 1907 she had taken out a substantial loan of £15,000. A few years later, there are records of her selling shares and parting with a couple of the precious violins in her musical

Great Warley. (Author's Collection)

museum – even taking in the occasional paying lodger. Not that this stopped her from spending excessive amounts of money on rare plants that she coveted for her precious gardens. She also enjoyed spending money on visiting royalty – although this was at least restricted to lunches and not to dinner parties or to overnight stays in the damp and draughty bedrooms. Another perverse economy was to replace her evening meal with a jug of Bovril.

Ellen Willmott was just as eccentric with regard to her security arrangements as her financial affairs. Having fired the night watchman after she caught him asleep, she installed a primitive system of alarm bells and hand bells to deter intruders. She even booby-trapped her daffodil fields. Now verging on paranoid, she also took to carrying a loaded revolver in her handbag should she attract attention on her late-night walks from Brentwood station.

The deterioration in Ellen's behaviour at this point drove Annie Cotterell away, tired of her employer's demands, her selfishness, rudeness and her suspicious nature. This left Robinson, her loyal and long-serving butler, in sole charge of the grand old house. The European properties had been sold, and it was now that both the Essex house and gardens began to deteriorate seriously.

Money was harder and harder to find – even Romford Council were pursuing her for non-payment of rates; such mercenary preoccupations doing nothing to restore the energetic equanimity associated with the younger Ellen Willmott. No one seemed to make an effort to visit her in her old age although she did still get involved in RHS affairs, and maintained her royal contacts, until the very end. A heart attack at seventy-six brought an end to her difficulties. After her death in 1934, there was talk of the gardens becoming a branch of Kew but the project was dropped on the outbreak of the Second World War. Instead, the house was sold for well over £11,000 and the gardens were plundered and vandalised. The site is now a nature reserve.

When the contents of Warley Place were sold, it was her collection of musical instruments that raised the most money. Her interest in music had been nearly as monumental as her interest in gardening. In the sale catalogue were items such as a gas-driven pipe organ, bagpipes, Arab tambourines, a Tibetan gong, a German hand-horn, shepherds' pipes from Egypt, drums, mandolins, guitars, lutes, zithers, pedal-harps, etc. – and it was said she could play them all.

'Miss Willmott's Ghost'.
(Author's Collection)

Ellen Willmott may not have been likeable, especially from middle age onwards. She may have looked after her plants while neglecting the needs of her staff and relatives. She was certainly regarded as selfish, bombastic, interfering and difficult to please. She may have been bitter in her solitude. But she left behind a valid, worthy and legendary contribution to horticulture. Over sixty plants have been named after her or her home at Warley. One in particular, 'Miss Willmott's Ghost' or *Eryngium giganteum*, is described as having been discreetly dispensed in the herbaceous borders of unwitting acquaintances by Ellen on her visits. By the time this thistle-like sea holly had 'mysteriously' flowered, her visit would have been forgotten. Without her, would there have been a Charlie Dimmock?

Frances Greville née Maynard, Countess of Warwick

1861–1938

When Daisy, as she was known, was just three years old, she inherited the Maynard family estates following the death of her father and grandfather. The inheritance centred around the sixteenth-century Easton Lodge, near Great Dunmow. This impressive residence was approached by a two-mile-long drive through 1,200 acres of parkland with deer roaming freely. It was here she spent most of her childhood with her mother, her sister Blanche and, later, her step-father, Lord Rosslyn. This is where she received the superficial but cultured education of the time, provided by governesses. As a result, Daisy was 'appropriately' knowledgeable in languages, reading, philosophy, music and the arts.

Fair-haired and blue-eyed, she grew up to be one of the great beauties of her age. As a result of this combination of stunning good looks and £30,000 a year, she was (in her own words) 'fêted, feasted, courted and adored', and in great demand as a marriage partner. She settled for Francis Greville, Lord Brooke, heir to the Earl of Warwick, turning down Prince Leopold – Queen Victoria's youngest son – along the

Easton Lodge. (Author's Collection)

way. They were married in Westminster Abbey in 1881, their wedding guests including the Prince and Princess of Wales, and one of their wedding gifts being a corrected copy of his own poems from Lord Tennyson.

Her life from here on was a round of country house parties, hunting, entertaining at her London home and flirting outrageously. Having produced an heir at the first attempt (born in September 1882) Daisy was thereafter able to return to her social whirl – with some relief it seems. Outside the hunting season, she became one of the local sights, driving a four-in-hand with consummate skill.

In 1886 – after another two children – she began an affair with Lord Charles Beresford, a dashing naval officer. Imagine her chagrin when she found out that his wife was pregnant (in 1889). The letter she wrote to Beresford in protest was opened by his wife, prompting the first of several scandals associated with Daisy.

The publicity does not seem to have deterred Edward, Prince of Wales, who is said to have switched his attentions from Lillie Langtry to 'Darling Daisy' at about this time. With royal influence behind her, Daisy put pressure on the fledgling railway company to provide a platform and 'station' at Little Easton for the prince to use. Such indiscretions were regarded as socially acceptable for someone of Daisy's class in the Victorian era, and her husband (Earl of Warwick from 1893) stood by her. An American magazine, the *World*, went so far as to claim that Lord Brooke could have named fourteen co-respondents if he had proceeded with a divorce, including the Duke of Marlborough and Lord Randolph Churchill. Later historians have counted Lord Rosebery, the Liberal Prime Minister, among her lovers. But divorce carried immense social stigma, and was not forthcoming.

She was also involved in a rather different scandal which reflected badly on the Prince of Wales when the story of Sir William Gordon-Cumming, a baronet of the Scots Guards, was leaked to the press. He had been caught cheating at baccarat and had sworn not to play cards again in return for full secrecy, as witnessed by the prince, who was now denounced as an immoral gambler. Daisy became known as 'Babbling Brooke' because of her inability to keep her extra-marital affairs private and here again she was accused of leaking the story, although she often denied this particular claim.

Although acquiring a reputation for philandering, Lady Warwick was not averse to assisting those from a less privileged background. She set up a needlework school at Easton for young women who could not handle the rough work of a farm or of domestic service, with a shop in London's Bond Street as an outlet for their work. Even this resulted in more troubles for her, as society despised 'trade'.

An even larger enterprise was Bigods School, near Dunmow, founded to provide agricultural and technical education for the middle classes in 1897. Daisy tried to interest the Prince of Wales in her philanthropy, but with little success. Their relationship had been giving his wife some concerns so the Prince of Wales replaced his 'own adored little Daisy wife' with Alice Keppel. In fact, Maynard, the son that Daisy bore some months later, has been accredited as the second son of the Earl of Warwick.

Maynard's embroidered baby clothes were made at the Easton school, which was producing exquisite workmanship. Daisy, after convalescing at Clacton with a bevy of nurses, made much more fuss of Maynard than she had of Guy (now fifteen and at Eton) and Marjorie (thirteen). It was around this period that she was also in demand as a sitter for a variety of portraits, photographs and sculptures.

A few years later, there is evidence of another affair – with a young army captain, Joseph Laycock, DSO, the son of a Conservative MP and five years her junior. Although they met at Warwick Castle, there are several examples of love letters from Daisy to Joseph in the Essex Record Office. One, dated 1902, suggests the secretive nature of their relationship as well as the depth of their – or at least her – commitment. It is headed up 6 a.m. and reads:

> My Darling, you will gather from this hour that I've not much time for writing but thank you so for the letter of Friday, and your wire was such a relief, as I have been so nervous of not doing as you wished . . . I simply long for a peaceful quiet Sunday because I feel that I understand everything that troubles you now, and I think things can be made clear between you and me for all time. It would be very unworthy of the great love I have for you if I was in any way a sorrow and worry to you . . . You see, I want all that is best for you Joe, and I know that with freedom your own fine character and splendid qualities will carry you over through everything. Only the woman who loves you best in the world and who has given her life to you understands too that she must sacrifice her own happiness and if need be her life to help you in the future whatever happens . . .

However, Laycock married someone else – Lady Downshire – in November of the year that she had written this letter. Daisy was particularly aggrieved by his ignoring her December birthday, and wrote some very different, angry letters at this point. The relationship does seem to have lasted a little longer, surviving the birth of his first child in November 1903, but finally her rather pathetic, pleading letters brought the relationship to an end. While it lasted, Laycock gave three scholarships to Bigods School and seems to have been happy to share in her self-appointed work, equipping the school workshop. (Essex County Council were only assisting to the tune of £100 per year.)

Affairs aside, her links with Warwickshire led Daisy to continue her philanthropic work in setting up another college for women, becoming a poor law guardian for Warwick and becoming interested in trade unionism. Back in Essex, she employed more than sixty men from the Salvation Army colony at Hadleigh to work on a newly-created 10-acre sunken garden at Easton designed by Harold Peto. The Salvation Army at this time was still a controversial movement and Daisy was seen to be patronising a rival non-Anglican church and to be encouraging 'wastrels'. In spite of gloomy local predictions, the men did a good job and were included in the Christmas dinner celebrations at Easton Lodge in 1902.

Certainly, Daisy's gradual conversion to socialism did not deter her from dressing as flamboyantly and expensively as she had always done when speaking out on behalf of the poor. Some considered her interest in socialism as attention-seeking, others considered her a traitor to her class.

Although even committed socialists had doubts about Daisy's commitment to the cause, she continued her involvement and started to write books and newspaper columns to boost the now ailing Warwick coffers. Funding the working class had not come cheaply and educational grants had stopped, necessitating the closure of Bigods in 1907, leaving Dunmow without a secondary school. She lost a considerable amount of money trying to start a newspaper, thanks to her gullible approach to investing, and sold some 20 acres for a few thousand pounds.

As 'lord of the manor' of Easton, she had the right of patronage of four local Essex parishes, enabling her to appoint socialist churchmen. The most controversial appointment was that of Conrad Noel, vicar of Thaxted, a committed Marxist. Less controversially, she turned a tithe barn in the grounds into a theatre, with a stage made by estate carpenters. This became another outlet for socialising – for whist drives and dances as well as theatricals. Ellen Terry, the actress of the day, performed here many times and became a good friend of Daisy.

She also had plenty of literary friends, including H.G. Wells, the controversial socialist and atheist, who she persuaded to collaborate with her on publishing Socialism and the Great State. In 1911, she rented the Little Easton Rectory, empty for some years, to Wells and his wife and two sons. He remained there until Jane Wells died in 1927, producing some sixty books in addition to articles. One semi-autobiographical novel, *Mr Britling Sees It Through*, was based on life in Little Easton during the First World War.

Daisy's financial situation prompted her to write her memoirs, including intimate correspondence with Edward VII when he was Prince of Wales. Not surprisingly, the royal family were anxious to maintain silence, and legal action ensured that these memoirs did not appear. Her silence also meant that many of her debts – as much as £48,000 – were mysteriously settled around this time by her financial advisor.

Little Easton church, 2007. (Author's Collection)

During the First World War, Lady Warwick found homes for Belgian refugees who were temporarily housed at Easton Lodge (in the barn), agreed for territorials to be trained on her land and sold venison at 6d per pound, thinning out her herd. She was able to speak in fluent German to prisoners of war in the Dunmow camp, a practice which unnerved the security guards. She closed the Easton estate to the local hunts, feeling that when so many were suffering, others should not be seeking pleasure – making her even more enemies. Her husband, as Lord Lieutenant of Essex, was involved in the training of the Essex regiments and defences.

Much of Easton Lodge was destroyed by a mysterious fire in the early morning of 22 February 1918. Lord and Lady Warwick and a few servants and pets were all evacuated safely. Interestingly, the original Elizabethan mansion had also been destroyed by fire in 1847. The loss of Daisy's letters and her amended memoirs was as much of a disaster as the loss of expensive clothes and jewellery. The west wing was rebuilt after the war at a cost of £27,000 and well over half the land Daisy had inherited was sold off.

But Lady Warwick continued to host gatherings of socialists and trade unionists at Easton, regardless of the fact that the estate was now in disrepair. In 1923, she offered to hand over the lodge to the Labour Party for conferences and study but they only took it on temporarily. In 1930 a series of weekend conferences were held at the lodge to revive socialism within the Labour Party itself, but her social extravagances were at an end – the money had run out. She was making some money from writing and translating, and she was still able to maintain quite a menagerie of animals – five hundred pet birds at one point, plus monkeys, peacocks, marmosets, dogs, cattle and even retired circus ponies. But when burglars broke in to Easton Lodge in January 1938, nothing seems to have been taken – probably because there was nothing of value left to take.

Remains of Easton Lodge, 2007. (Author's Collection)

After a busy and flamboyant life, Daisy had begun to tire of Essex. She deplored the coming of the motor car, driven at what she considered wild and dangerous speeds, and felt besieged by day-trippers peering through her park gates or gaping at the mansion. Although she threatened to move to the west coast of Scotland, Daisy died at Easton Lodge in July 1938 with Maynard in attendance.

Lord Warwick had died over ten years earlier while staying at Beer in Devon, where there is a tablet to his memory in the local church. The family vault is, however, at Warwick. Maynard, Daisy's surviving son, inherited just £37,000, a fraction of the wealth that Daisy herself had inherited. Another fire damaged Easton Lodge in 1946 and it was demolished in 1947, the grounds already pretty much destroyed when they were turned into an airfield during the Second World War. (Note that soldiers were billeted here during the Second World War and told stories of a shrouded figure descending the grand staircase – for those of you who believe in ghosts.)

Over 1,500 acres of woodland, farmland and part of the gardens remained in the Maynard family until 2004, when the estate was sold to Land Securities plc. Some parts of the garden remain open to visitors to this day and there is an impressive marble bust in St Mary's church at nearby Little Easton. The unusual sculpture in the grounds, by Anna Schwegmann-Fielding, is created from objects unearthed from the gardens over the years. Anna regards the sculpture as a kind of mini-museum, with Daisy's delicate frame adorned with bullet cases, shells, handles, crockery and clay pipes, each with their own story to tell. At the centre of her chest, hidden within a blue ceramic daisy, a profile of Edward VII can just be seen. It is a tactile, striking and fitting image.

Above: Countess of Warwick sculpture, Easton Lodge. (Courtesy of Douglas Atfield); *Image of 'Darling Daisy' inset into sculpture.* (Author's Collection)

Ladies of the Road

Nineteenth & Twentieth Centuries

Some of these ladies had a brief spell of infamy, in quite a different class to royal mistresses or suffragettes from comfortable backgrounds. While establishing biographical information about the homeless is virtually impossible, the little that is available is of interest in showing the range of women that have made Essex, in some ways, the infamous county it is today.

In the 1880s, two such ladies in their forties were known around Colchester as the 'Silly Hannahs'. It is not known for sure whether they were sisters, or even twins,

The Silly Hannahs. (Courtesy of Patrick Denney)

though this seems possible. They slept rough, and made money for food by selling goods made out of rushes – mats and baskets.

The elder walked ahead of the younger, adopting rather a regal pose in the manner of some kind of queen (or, allegedly, an Indian princess) and wearing a pile of hats on her head. She would always ask anyone who purchased goods if they had an unwanted hat for her collection, which just grew and grew. By 1900, they were dependent on charity. Once one of them died, the other was taken into the Colchester workhouse.

* * *

Moving on to the beginning of the twentieth century, Jane Carpenter, a decrepit seventy-eight-year-old tramp, was in the news when she accused Sergeant Walter Peters of assaulting her. The assault – if such it was – took place in Chelmsford at the junction of Wood Street and London Road, on the beat of patrolling constables. Mrs Carpenter claimed that she had stretched out on a seat located at the junction, after refreshing herself with cold potatoes and beer at a local pub and after collecting her admission ticket to Chelmsford workhouse. A local worthy, Frederick Taylor, heard her cries of pain and saw Sergeant Peters walking away.

Taylor brought Peters back to the seat where the tramp was still howling, claiming the constable had kicked her when she refused to show him her workhouse ticket. She showed her bloodstained underclothing to the growing audience, and Sergeant Peters escorted her to the workhouse. But it didn't end there, because Taylor arranged for Jane Carpenter to be examined the next day – revealing bruised and cut buttocks. He raised the £50 needed to privately prosecute Peters for causing grievous bodily

Chelmsford Union workhouse, now St John's Hospital. (John Drury)

harm, because he obviously felt strongly about the case. Taylor does not, however, seem to have had a lot of local support, the general feeling being that a policeman was incapable of committing a crime.

When the case came to court, the trial was dominated by evidence which favoured Peters. The Chelmsford Union workhouse doctor was not convinced that the injuries Mrs Carpenter had received were in accord with her description of the assault, and the blood was not 'fresh' enough to support her story. Other witnesses felt that she was drunk, and that there was no evidence of blood on the sergeant's boots, as would have been the case if the story was true. An earlier disagreement between Peters and Taylor – regarding a theatrical performance Taylor, obviously a prominent citizen, had organised – was brought into the equation to suggest that Taylor still bore a grievance.

Jane Carpenter did not help her situation with her inconsistent evidence. She took the stand dressed in union-house garb, 'sunburnt and wrinkled', and admitted to a number of previous convictions including a sentence of seven years penal servitude. There was even an earlier allegation of indecent assault against a policeman. Her descriptions of the assault varied – he used a boot, then a stick; she was sitting down, lying down, standing up; she had 'perhaps' been knocked down earlier by a car (which could have caused the injuries) as witnessed by another local man.

The case was dismissed as involving too much doubt. It had not even been necessary to call the witnesses who had attended to give evidence in Peters' favour. Jane Carpenter was provided with food and returned to the union workhouse. Mr Taylor seems to have been instrumental in providing her with a cab to Shenfield station and was probably the man (unnamed in the *Essex County Chronicle*) who purchased a ticket to London for her. She disappeared from Essex and Peters retired in 1908, reputation intact.

* * *

Before the First World War, 'Marmalade Emma' Taylor was well known as a vagrant (or traveller) in the Colchester and Blackheath area. Little is known of her background, other than that she came from Great Horkesley and was allegedly the daughter of a Brightlingsea mariner. She would wear floor-length, old-fashioned, cast-off dresses or skirts with a thick tweed jacket on top to hide her cat, which seemed to spend a lot of time curled up inside. A couple of cooking pots would be fastened to a rope at her waist. Atop this vision was a straw hat, lavishly decorated with ribbons, ostrich feathers in the winter and flowers in the summer, her hair in long black plaits beneath. As a finishing touch, there was a clay pipe clamped between her lips.

She is believed to have acquired her name from her fondness for marmalade. Although another version of its origin suggests that she

Marmalade Emma.
(Courtesy of Patrick Denney)

dropped a jar of marmalade in one of Colchester's narrow shopping streets (Wyre Street) which smashed to pieces, prompting calls of 'Marmalade! Emma!' Her companion was another vagrant known as Teddy Grimes and they seemed quite fond of each other. Emma sometimes referred to herself as Mrs Grimes but it seems doubtful that they were actually married. They spent their days begging for food – including food for the cat – and their nights sleeping rough in ditches or haystacks, in woods or spinneys, even in the snow. The wood fires they made up would have been used as much for a little extra warmth as to warm up any scraps they had managed to beg. They sometimes managed to spend a night in a local blacksmiths (much warmer) or on a local farm.

Emma was put into prison at least once – for using foul language to a policeman. She had a reputation for using foul language to deter the approach of young children, many of whom were frightened of her, although she kept herself to herself unless teased. Legend has it that upon her release, she boasted that she had been to 'college'. Another story is of her smuggling her cat into Essex County Hospital when she was admitted for treatment (probably for a bronchial problem) and putting up quite a fight to keep it before it was finally removed to more suitable temporary accommodation.

Eventually, Emma and Teddy went to live on a derelict barge on the River Colne, which at least provided some shelter in bad weather. This is where she ended her days, in about 1920. Both of these characters are buried in a paupers' grave in Colchester churchyard.

There are many other stories out there, but they have not been written into history. For instance, in just one month of 1906 (January), 312 vagrants are listed as applying for poor relief at Colchester Borough police station, many of these women. Such applications often resulted in a spell in the workhouse – of which there were many throughout Essex. As a result of the Poor Law Act of 1837, food and shelter were provided as an obligation on the part of workhouses, but the accommodation provided was inferior, lacking ventilation.

Although nineteenth-century statistics (as in Henry Mayhew's 1851 *London Labour and the London Poor*) proved that a third of criminals came from the vagrant classes, such statistics focus on the male population. While these Essex women were reviled and achieved temporary notoriety for their lifestyles, is the truth rather that they were just desperate to survive?

A homeless child.
(Author's Collection)

Amy Bull née Hicks

1877–1953

Amy – and her mother – were not as well known as the Pankhursts, but were equally committed to the suffragette cause, and equally militant. Amy was born at Great Holland Hall, not far from Frinton-on-Sea, the daughter of Charles and Lilian Hicks. Luckily for Amy, Charles, a farmer, believed in educating his daughters as well as his only son, and she graduated from Cambridge in 1899 with a first-class degree in classics.

Her mother, born in Colchester, worked for the suffragette movement from the 1880s and was involved in the 1884 agitation over the agricultural labourers' vote, so it is not too surprising that she too became involved in the movement from the outset.

By 1902 mother and daughter were members of the Central Society for Women's Suffrage, later joining the Women's Social and Political Union (WSPU) and the Women's Freedom League. Amy became secretary for the WFL in 1909 and was imprisoned in July of that year for three weeks on a charge of obstruction. She was a founder member of the Tax Resistance League and twice had her goods distrained in lieu of unpaid tax. She was arrested again (with her mother) the following year during the struggle with the police in Parliament Square, a November day known as Black Friday.

Lilian Hicks organised a number of meetings in the Great Holland area but, in an interview in *The Vote* in 1910, described it as having been an 'uphill' battle to get anyone to attend. She said that she had the impression that a keen Woman's Suffragist was, until the twentieth century, 'looked upon as a crank of the first water'. By the time of this interview, however, the Royal Albert Hall was starting to host suffrage meetings on a rather grander scale. She also refers to being denied the opportunity to figure in the list of 'her country's criminals' and wear 'the broad arrow' because some 'mysterious and anonymous agent' had paid her fine of 40s when she was sentenced to a fine or seven days in prison as a result of taking part in a deputation to Mr Asquith in 1909. It seems that Lilian would have been honoured to join the list which contained 'the names of some of the noblest women of our time'.

Great Holland. (Author's Collection)

Above: Runsell Green. (Author's Collection)

Right: Lilian Hicks. (Photograph by Lena Connell, supplied by Museum of London Picture Library)

As a result of Amy's involvement in the window-smashing campaign initiated by the WSPU in the West End in 1912, she spent four months in Holloway and Aylesbury prisons. Some of her time was spent in solitary confinement, and she was probably one of the ringleaders of the hunger strikers at Aylesbury, resulting in her being forcibly fed. Her mother, Lilian, 'escaped' again, being acquitted of window-smashing.

Amy lived at Runsell Green, Danbury, not far from Chelmsford, during the 1920s. In 1927 she married John Major Bull, a widower twenty years older than she. The couple were high-profile, he in the War Office, and she as a rural district councillor in Chelmsford from her marriage until 1930. Her husband died in 1944 and she saw out her days at General's Orchard, Little Baddow, near Chelmsford, dying there of pneumonia in 1953.

There is a catalogue in the Essex Record Office in Chelmsford which gives fascinating detail of the contents of General's Orchard, which were sold at auction in a marquee on the premises. The contents of ten bedrooms were sold, plus a workshop, a morning room, drawing room, dining room, library, billiards room, kitchen, and maid's sitting room. The most money raised was £300 for a Queen Anne suite with six chairs and settee, the lowest being just 1s for a mattress. Other items epitomise the period – a Gladstone bag, mahogany washstands, inlaid lacquered cabinet, leather-bound books (some in Latin and including Shakespeare, Homer and Byron), a coal scuttle, a gramophone, and even a canoe and paddles. In all there were 378 lots.

So nothing remains of Amy and the childless life she lived in Essex. Except that her militancy paid off with the 1918 Representation of the People Act, giving votes to women over thirty, albeit not on the same terms as men (they had to be either wives of householders or graduates) and all women over twenty-one finally got the vote in 1928. The methodology may have been violent, but the outcome was exactly the result that Amy, her mother and her contemporaries had fought for.

Sylvia Pankhurst

1882–1960

The name Sylvia Pankhurst will certainly be known to Essex and non-Essex readers alike, but her Essex connection is not as well known. She was not necessarily the most violent in the Pankhurst suffragette family and her infamy is as much from the life she led after the First World War as it is from her political activity.

It is not that surprising that Sylvia, Christabel and Adela grew up with radical views. Their father was a highly educated barrister with political ambitions within the Liberal party, and their mother, Emmeline, twenty-four years his junior, was keener on playing a role in public life than on domestic duties. Sylvia had a comfortable middle-class childhood, spent in Manchester, Southport and in Russell Square, London, but she had her first contact with Essex when sent on a lengthy summer holiday to a boarding house in Clacton in 1891 with her nurse and her siblings. Note the absence of parents.

Sylvia Pankhurst.
(International Newsreel NY)

The children grew up quickly, treated as young adults by their parents. They were showered with books, not toys, as they matured. Sadly for the family – and especially for Emmeline – the two boys died at young ages, Frank in 1888 at just four (diphtheria) and Harry in 1910 at twenty-one from polio – unlike the three sisters who all made it well past their three score and ten. Their push into adulthood was exacerbated by the death of their father in 1898. Although forced to downsize to a less favourable part of Manchester, they retained a family servant, and Emmeline secured paid employment at the Registrar of Births and Deaths to assist the family fortunes.

By 1902, Christabel and her mother were already involved in the early suffrage society, although Sylvia seemed more interested in art at this stage, and won a scholarship to study mosaics in Venice, a city she fell in love with. But she returned a year later to help her mother to decorate a newly built Socialist hall in Salford, funded by a memorial fund to her father.

After winning another scholarship to the Royal College of Art in South Kensington, she met Keir Hardie, co-founder of the Independent Labour Party, who helped her to eke a living by selling some commercial art and writing articles and books, keeping her away from the possibility of real poverty. Before their friendship, she had been lonely in the big city, and there is quite a bit of evidence to indicate that they became lovers, probably her first sexual experience. He almost certainly reminded Sylvia of her father, being many years her senior, and he had a taste for female company when away from his wife in Ayrshire. All indications, from surviving letters between the two, are that the affair, although low-profile, lasted until at least 1912, just a few years before he died.

Sylvia's activities within the Women's Social and Political Union were rather more limited than those of Emmeline and Christabel, who had moved their centre of operation to London. However, Sylvia was still involved, having taken part in demonstrations including one at the opening of Parliament in October 1906 which resulted in her imprisonment, along with her sister Adela and nine other leading suffragettes. From then onwards, Sylvia was always in the thick of the fight. In February 1907 Sylvia was in prison again following the WSPU demonstration at the opening of Parliament, when she and her fellow militants had been confronted by mounted police, an over-reaction denounced in the press. It was in fact Sylvia who, as the suffragettes travelled the country to drum up support, wrote down her observations on the way women were being treated in factories and mines, and strengthening her socialist views, antagonising her conservative family.

In the meantime, her young brother Harry, frail and gentle, was struggling to find his own niche in society. He was despatched to Mayland in Essex to work in the open air on the smallholdings there, Emmeline seeming to think that fresh air was a cure-all for physical weakness. However, Harry seems to have taken advantage of one of Emmeline's spells of incarceration by finding himself a job at a sanatorium run by a woman doctor, but the doctor could see that he was not a healthy individual and even offered to take him as a patient. Emmeline, when freed, packed him back off to Essex. Not long after, Harry developed a bladder complaint, and spent several months in a nursing home while his mother embarked on an American tour. This illness (which in fact seems to have been undiagnosed polio) left him partly paralysed, and in pain. Sylvia visited him regularly, but the drugs he was on finally saw him drift from unconsciousness to death, devastating his mother who declared that she wanted to be buried with her two sons when her own time came.

The 1912/13 violence – smashing windows, setting fire to pillar boxes – distanced Sylvia even further from the way the WSPU was going, and she opted to organise a branch (the East London Federation) to effectively resurrect its original, non-violent methodology to achieve votes for women. She was also able to launch the *Woman's Dreadnought*, whose libellous copy did not prevent it surviving until 1924, after changing its name to the *Workers' Dreadnought*. Her own campaigning was assisted by close co-operation with high-profile male suffragists, but it did not prevent her being arrested and imprisoned eight times between 1913 and 1914, in spite of her varying attempts to disguise herself.

Sylvia was often forcibly fed, using a method sometimes used on contemporary 'lunatics'. Various types of liquid food, Valentine's meat juice, Benger's food or beef tea were pumped into the prisoner's stomach through a rubber tube fixed in the mouth or nostrils. Contemporary reporting reveals that six or seven wardresses were needed to hold a girl down while this was being done, and it could be very dangerous if any of the liquid was forced into the lungs. She wrote of women also enduring rectal feeding, and of being drugged with bromides and hallucinogens. A debilitating experience for a woman who was essentially artistic. Well over a hundred doctors signed a petition protesting about the use of force-feeding, but to little effect it seems. Several

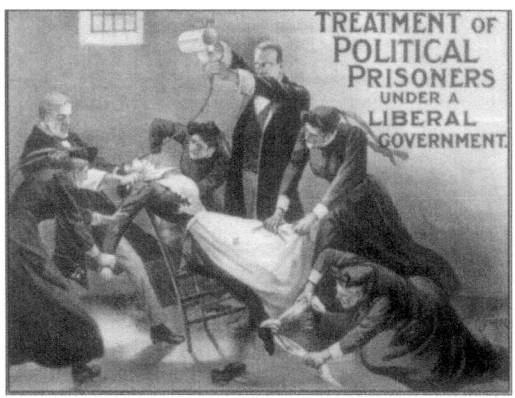
Image of suffragette. (Rockwell Cards)

suffragettes, including Sylvia, also used sleep deprivation to draw attention to their plight, publicly damaging their health to the fury and frustration of the prison authorities.

In spite of her sufferings in the cause of women's suffrage, the two organisations (the ELF and the WSPU) had so many disagreements about the way forward that they split officially early in 1914. Adela, too, sharing some of Sylvia's left-wing opinions, was 'cut off' from the Pankhursts and sent to Australia – where women had already won the vote – with £20, enough to enable her to make a start in a different country where she could focus on something new: equal rights.

After the outbreak of the First World War, Sylvia became something of a local heroine in London's East End, establishing clinics, milk distribution, an employment exchange, a nursery, even a garment factory paying better than average weekly wages. However, in spite of this, her pacifist leanings were not popular – East Enders wanted to defeat the Germans, not negotiate a peace. Sylvia began to lose heart, not helped by the death of her beloved Keir Hardie in 1915. The *Dreadnought* moved away from local, East London issues to national ideological questions.

Once the war was over, Sylvia felt able to pursue her interest in Marxism and she played a controversial part in getting the British Communist Party off the ground in 1920 – in spite of growing financial difficulties. But it was to be domesticity rather than politics that brought her to Essex, when Silvio Corio came into her life.

They met during the war, sharing common ground with their anarchical political views. Silvio gathered material for publication in Sylvia's *Dreadnought*. By the time Sylvia was forced to sell her commercial headquarters in the Old Ford Road in the East End (1923), and was obliged to cease production of the *Dreadnought*, they had become lovers. Sylvia bought a small ramshackle 300-year-old property in Woodford Wells, and Silvio became a regular visitor. Unsurprisingly, the house was christened Red Cottage.

To help with her finances, Sylvia decided to open a tea room, given the cottage's location opposite a public house which attracted swarms of summer visitors on their way to and from Epping Forest. A good idea in principle, except that Sylvia had never had to cater for anyone – not even for herself. It meant that she had to buy cakes to sell on, diminishing the potential profits. Luckily, Silvio was able to cook when he was around, and he grew vegetables, built a greenhouse and an outside seating area for customers. Friends from the East End all seem to have been willing to help out, and Sylvia became reliant on their unpaid assistance. As a result, the income was a welcome supplement to her earnings from writing.

Certainly her mother seems to have been inspired by Sylvia's modest success, because she left Bermuda where she had been living in the 1920s and opened a teashop in France. This venture, in Juan les Pins, failed dismally, leaving Emmeline, at sixty-seven, with four adopted young daughters, no regular income and a disinclination to get involved in pressurising Stanley Baldwin to extend the 1918 Reform Act by reducing the age when women could vote from thirty to twenty-one. She was content with what she had achieved – but not for long, since she became allied to the Conservative Party on her return to England in 1926, a great disappointment for Sylvia.

At forty-five, and now living openly with Silvio, Sylvia made an unexpected decision to become a mother. The question of marriage did not arise – it suited neither her nor Silvio, who already had at least two illegitimate children by different mothers. There was also a legal complication at the time in that as the wife of a foreign national (Silvio was Italian) she was in danger of forfeiting her rights as a British citizen.

Her pregnancy did nothing to heal the breach between Sylvia and her mother. In fact, Emmeline is alleged to have referred to her daughter as that 'scarlet woman' when Sylvia called to see her during her pregnancy. She even accused Sylvia of deliberately trying to humiliate her. Unmarried motherhood in the 1920s was bound to be a considerable embarrassment when linked to such a high-profile political figure.

Richard Keir Pethick Pankhurst was born in December 1927 in a London nursing home. Sylvia, retreating to Red Cottage, made no attempt to keep his birth under wraps, however. She was happy to talk to, even encourage, journalists, and even the *News of the World* headlined the story as a 'new sensation' – especially as Sylvia did not name the father and criticised her family for ostracising her. Emmeline was actually living close by when Richard was just a few months old, staying with friends in Chipping Ongar. Six months later, in declining health, she was removed to a London nursing home but survived for just a few more days. Just one month before her death, the legislation had been passed giving the vote to women on equal terms with men.

Emmeline's London funeral was the only occasion after the war when all three sisters met up. Sylvia returned to the struggle of trying to earn a living from her writing, but Christabel and Adela returned to their adopted countries, the USA and Australia respectively. Some of Sylvia's articles, published in the *Evening Standard* and the Star, were attempts to ensure that her own role was not marginalised.

Meanwhile, Sylvia had been left some land at Bradwell-on-Sea and sold this to enable her to move from the Red Cottage to a larger, three-storey house in Charteris Road, Woodford. West Dene was big enough to enable her and Silvio to install printing machinery, and there was enough space to rent out the top floor as a flat.

Even with these improvements to her finances, it was difficult for Sylvia to maintain a proficient writing output while coping with a young child who needed much of her attention. Silvio was not always around, and, in any case, was a sciatica sufferer, so not able to be of too much assistance with young Richard. Housework, it seems, was not a priority, as Richard recalled at a much later date.

Sylvia was now something of a local eccentric – a vegetarian (not that common in the 1930s), untidy, keeping very late hours in her study, keen on writing books that reflected her Marxist views, her interest in an international language or in denouncing British imperialism, especially in India. She started a Montessori school in Charteris Road that benefited the local community as well as providing some additional care for Richard. She also began to write more accessible books about motherhood, as well as perhaps her most famous work, *The Suffragette Movement*, published in 1931. Even with literary success, her income was not keeping up with her outgoings.

The rise of fascism in Europe gave Sylvia and Silvio something else to worry about, and again they started a newspaper – an anti-fascist one which had a circulation of

40,000 at its peak (the *New Times and Ethiopian News*). Their views on the fascist menace were confirmed in 1939 and two Anderson shelters appeared promptly in the garden of Charteris Road. Not unnaturally, the couple concerned themselves with securing the release of anti-fascist Italians from internment. Such was their involvement, that Sylvia – mainly because of her newspaper, newly subtitled *The National Anti-Fascist Weekly* – received death threats, and she was given police protection as a result. But her work was appreciated by no less than Emperor Haile Selassie who invited her to Ethiopia for a protracted visit during 1944–5, during which she was awarded several medals for her support over unification.

Upon returning to Essex, Sylvia found plenty to write about after the war, given her ongoing criticism of British government at home and overseas. She was interviewed as late as 1952 when she was seventy, the journalist concerned describing her as having an Edwardian look.

Her son took on more of her work as he grew older, with Silvio still taking a back seat, and now taking on less and less activity. During the 1950s, Richard was named as joint author of at least two of Sylvia's lengthy books on the history of Ethiopia, though these were more propaganda than academic. As her work began to take its toll, she tried to deflect a nervous breakdown by staying for a few weeks in the nearby Royal Forest Hotel, but, upon returning home, she had her first heart attack in 1953. In 1954, there were mixed turning points in her life – Silvio died, aged eighty, and Haile Selassie came to Britain to receive an honorary degree at Oxford, one of several ceremonies in his honour which Sylvia attended.

But Sylvia did not stay on in Essex for much longer. She and Richard went to Ethiopia in 1956, and she was in no hurry to return, being disappointed with what women were doing with their hard-won voting power. She sold her house in Woodford before leaving, taking only her white Persian cat – the contents of the house were auctioned off. She had no need of them in the residence in Addis Ababa she was offered by the emperor. This sprawling bungalow, with the addition of a handful of servants and a sweet-smelling garden, became her final home.

Richard married a Romanian girl that he had met in London, and they too settled in the Ethiopian house, Richard eventually becoming the Director of the Institute of Ethiopian Studies. Sylvia continued to work, writing for the *Ethiopian Observer*. She had never really learned what to do with her leisure time. She spent her last years helping others, involved in setting up medical services and employment exchanges, and this seemed to have satisfied her even more than her work with the suffragettes. When she died, aged seventy-eight, she was in the middle of fund-raising for a maternity wing in Addis Ababa. Her passing was an event of national importance in Ethiopia, but marked only with a dutiful service at Caxton Hall in England.

Infamous for her militant anarchy, her hunger strikes, her strong views and her lifestyle – 'living in sin' with a 'foreigner' and producing an illegitimate child – Sylvia Pankhurst should nevertheless be a name to make Essex more proud than ashamed of her connection. She was responsible for the creation of the stone Anti-Air War Memorial which stood on Woodford Green, and her name lives on in Pankhurst Green near Woodford station, which sports a very low-key memorial plaque.

Edith Thompson

1893–1923

Edith was a Christmas day baby, born in Dalston to a working-class couple who soon moved to traffic-free Manor Park to accommodate the growing family. As an artistic, attractive teenager with impressive auburn locks, she turned quite a few heads, but was pursued most ardently by Percy Thompson – it seems they met in about 1909 during their regular commute to their London jobs. The fact that Edith resisted Percy's marriage proposals for some six years (until she was twenty-one) perhaps indicates that she was not entirely sure that she had found the love of her life, although there was no doubt they had become lovers during this long courtship.

Even her wedding day in 1916, overshadowed by the war and Percy's imminent conscription, saw her in doubt as to whether she would actually go through with the wedding, but what she did enjoy was the whole drama of the occasion. Their honeymoon at Southend-on-Sea seems to have been a success, and Edith was immensely cheered by the fact that Percy was, soon after, honourably discharged as unfit for active service because of a heart condition – she wouldn't be a war widow. It does seem that the hypochondriac Percy 'suffered' from little other than surplus weight allied to a heavy smoking habit . . . and it is also quite likely that he deliberately fooled the army's medical officers.

Even so, after a year living with Edith's parents, the couple moved to the healthier air of Westcliff-on-Sea. They rented a furnished flat at 25 Retreat Road, near the station, allowing them to commute to jobs in London, where the air raids continued until 1918. Once the end of the war had been announced, they realised how much they missed the social side of London life, and stayed with Percy's relatives while house-hunting in Ilford. Edith was earning more than Percy as a skilled book-keeper and buyer for a London fashion house, and they could afford to buy their first house – at 41 Kensington Gardens, christened The Retreat after their Westcliff home.

No. 25 Retreat Road, Westcliff-on-Sea, 2007. (Author's Collection)

Her meeting with Freddy Bywaters was early in January 1920. He was a self-assured, young seaman – just seventeen years old – and was acquainted with her brothers. Percy foolishly assumed that Freddy was interested in Edith's sister, Avis, and, even more foolishly, invited him on holiday with the three of them during the hot summer of 1921. This trip to the Isle of Wight almost certainly sowed the seeds of the illicit relationship between Edith and Freddy.

Freddy was invited by Percy to join the Thompsons in their Ilford home as a paying guest, joining tenants already installed. At this point, Freddy became deliberately landlocked. This enabled him to spend more time with Edith, and, finally, Percy became suspicious and the arguments started, eventually driving Freddy from the house.

This did not, of course, resolve the situation. The lovers went on meeting, and Percy became more aggressive in his manner towards his wife. He could not stop her writing letters to Freddy, however, most of which Freddy seemed to have kept, and which proved so significant at their trials.

While Freddy was back at sea, he sent his letters to Edith's workplace. She was not always happy with their content, finding them less affectionate than she would have liked, and, perhaps as a direct result, the Thompsons do seem to have resumed a marital sex life. She aborted Percy's child in January 1922, apparently without his knowledge, shortly after Freddy's return from overseas.

Edith and Freddy snatched what time they could while he was on shore leave, but the letters continued even before he had to leave yet again. At her suggestion, Freddy had provided Edith with quinine and she wrote to him of an attempt to poison Percy by putting the quinine in his tea, telling him that, as this failed, she would try crushing glass in his food instead. Such claims would be dismissed as fantasies in due course, but are undoubtedly incriminating.

Freddy Bywaters' last sailing was in June 1922 when he set off for a fifteen-week trip to Australia – much longer than his earlier separations from Edith. During this trip, Edith is alleged to have aborted for a second time, this baby likely to have been Freddy's. The lovers used a post office address for their continuing correspondence, Edith being 'Miss Fisher', because Percy had realised that Edith was receiving letters at her work address.

The tenor of the correspondence would suggest, however, that Freddy was cooling, and it could well be that his thoughts were turning back in the direction of her less-complicated sister, Avis. Not that he had ever claimed to be totally faithful to Edith, and she had also had her admirers, although it is less likely that she had sexual relationships with them. Even Percy, in defeat, was rumoured to have started looking elsewhere for female companionship.

However, the physical intensity of their reunion in September after such a long spell apart, followed by a visit to Wanstead Park for a passionate sexual coupling, diminished any mutual doubts they may have had. Their letters after this reunion were some of the lengthiest they had yet produced, full of declarations of love.

On Tuesday 3 October 1922, the fateful day arrived. Around midnight, Edith and Percy were walking home from Ilford station after an evening at the theatre. Freddy was following them, unacknowledged by Edith, perhaps even without her knowledge, until, close to home, Freddy rushed out, knife in hand, pushing Edith aside. After a scuffle, Percy was stabbed a number of times in the body and neck. As Edith ran to his

Pre-war Ilford. (Author's Collection)

aid, Freddy bolted, undoubtedly recognised by Edith by this point. Neighbours who had heard Edith's screams appeared, and a local doctor and then an ambulance were called out to what was now a dead body. Edith at this juncture seems to have been incoherent, suggesting that her husband had had some kind of seizure, and making no reference to an assailant.

It was a simple job for the police to recognise that this was a murder they were handling. By lunchtime the next day Edith was helping the police with their enquiries at Ilford police station. A few hours later, Freddy, too, was in custody, by which time he would have seen the national newspapers and the story of the 'murdered shipping clerk' at Ilford – so he would have known that Percy was dead and not just badly injured. He seemed to come over as insolent in protesting his innocence, but it was again simple for the police to find plenty of evidence against him – his bloodied clothes (at his mother's home in Upper Norwood) and the scores of letters he had kept there from Edith for a start.

While their initial statements denied all knowledge of murder, Edith, having glimpsed Freddy at the station and assumed he was there to confess, changed her statement to admitting that she saw Freddy attack her husband. Freddy, shown her admission, then changed his statement too, denying Edith's involvement in his attack on Percy, and claiming his intent to injure rather than kill.

The press had a field day. Edith was decried as a wicked and debauched adulteress, an abortionist, the 'Messalina of Ilford', corrupting a mere boy and mistreating her inoffensive husband. At the trial, the solicitor-general made a number of references to passages in Edith's letters which could be interpreted as conspiracy to murder. Edith had also sent Freddy clippings cut from newspapers of cases of poisoning, and there were references to her having tried putting ground glass in her husband's tea,

Press coverage of Edith Thompson's trial. (*Illustrated London News*, 1922, courtesy of John Weedy)

foiled when Percy had complained of its bitterness. Fantasy? Perhaps. Circumstantial evidence? Certainly. But, for a jury – convincing.

Freddy and Edith, when giving evidence, pointed out Percy's mistreatment of Edith, and Freddy also stated that Percy had threatened to shoot him. Such a belated plea of self-defence, offset by the tone and content of Edith's letters, did not wash with the Old Bailey jury who took just two hours to find them both guilty. It is not difficult to see why, given just one line in what was perhaps her last letter: 'You are jealous of him, but I want you to be . . . be jealous so that you will do something desperate.' In 1922, the death sentence was not unexpected.

Predictably, both appealed. A letter was published from Freddy's mother, broken-hearted at the prospect of losing her son, following the death of her husband during the First World War, having given 'his life for you and yours'. This led to the largest petition ever signed in Great Britain, Freddy seemingly having attracted more sympathy that Edith . . . but to no avail. Edith spent her last Christmas – and birthday – in Holloway prison.

In January 1923, the lovers were separated for ever. Freddy's hanging at Pentonville was less traumatic than Edith's at Holloway. She had to be sedated, her hands and ankles tied, and she had to be carried to the site. The hanging of Edith is recorded elsewhere in grim, repugnant detail, leading to the eventual suicide of the executioner, and the retirement of the prison governor and chaplain. Her last words? 'I am not guilty.' So, if she knew nothing about Freddy's attack on Percy, which he maintained to the end was an impulsive action undertaken when he was drunk, was she in fact hanged for the immoral life she was perceived to have led?

Postscript: A wax reproduction of Edith and Freddy was a popular attraction for some years at Madame Tussaud's. Her actual remains, along with several others, were removed from Holloway Prison when it was being redeveloped in 1971 and she was reinterred in Brookwood Cemetery, Surrey.

Conclusion

While it has been interesting to research and write about such a diverse range of interesting Essex women from all walks of life, readers should not close this book with the impression that these ladies are necessarily representative of the county. There are a whole lot of worthwhile Essex women out there – philanthropists, academics, campaigners and martyrs, medics and writers, musicians and even a few saints. Enough, certainly, for another book.

The modern, twenty-first century Essex Girl is often belittled, but, for every negative image, there is a positive one out there.

Bibliography

Addison, William, *Epping Forest*, Robert Hale, London, 1991
Addison, William, *Essex Heyday*, J.M. Dent & Sons, London, 1949
Addison, William, *Essex Worthies*, Phillimore & Co. Ltd, Chichester, 1973
Barnes, Alison, *Essex Eccentrics*, Boydell Press, Ipswich, 1975
Bingley, Randal, *Fobbing Life and Landscape*, Lejins Publishing, Stanford-le-Hope, 1997
Blunden, Margaret, *The Countess of Warwick*, Cassell & Co Ltd, London, 1967
Butler, Iris, *Rule of Three*, Hodder and Stoughton Ltd, London, 1967
Butler, Ivan, *Murderers' England*, Robert Hale, London, 1973
Buttery, David, *Portraits of a Lady*, Brewin Books, Studley, 1988
Chapman, Hester W., *Two Tudor Portraits*, Cedric Chivers Ltd, Bath, 1973
Clark, Roy, *The Harwich Death Club*, Essex Police History Notebook No. 11, Chelmsford, undated
Clarke, Mary Anne, *Authentic and Interesting Memoirs of Mrs Clarke*, David Longworth, Boston, 1809
Colthorpe, Marion & Bateman, Linley H., *Queen Elizabeth I & Harlow*, Harlow Development Corporation, 1977
Denney, Patrick, *Colchester Past*, Ian Henry Publications, Romford, 1988
Donaldson, William, *Brewer's Rogues, Villains & Eccentrics*, Cassell, London, 2002
Donnelley, Paul, *Essex Murders*, Wharncliffe Books, Barnsley, 2007
Eastment, Winifred, *Wanstead through the Ages*, Essex Countryside (Books), Letchworth, 1946
Elizabethan Essex (no author) published by Essex Record Office, Chelmsford, Publication no. 34, 1961
Essex Countryside numerous issues
Essex Life numerous issues
Essex Review numerous issues
Essex Weekly News numerous issues
Evans, Brian, *Romford Heritage*, Sutton Publishing Ltd, Stroud, 2002
Fitch, E.A., *Maldon and the River Blackwater*, Gowers Ltd, Maldon, c. 1912
Godwin, William, *Memoirs of the Author of a Vindication of the Rights of Woman*, J. Johnson, London, 1798
Gordon, Dee, *People Who Mattered in Southend and Beyond*, Ian Henry Publications, Romford, 2006
Gray, Adrian, *Crime and Criminals in Victorian Essex*, Countryside Books, Newbury, 1988

Gray, Adrian, *Tales of Old Essex*, Countryside Books, Newbury, 1987
Hendy, Phyl, *The St Osyth Witch Story*, self-published, 2003
Hope, T.M., *An Essex Pie*, Benham & Co., Colchester, 1951
Jacobs, Diane, *The Life of Mary Wollstonecraft*, Abacus, London, 2001
Jarvis, Stan, *Essex Murder Casebook*, Countryside Books, Newbury, 1994
Jarvis, Stan, *Essex Pride*, Ian Henry Publications, Romford, 1984
Jarvis, Stan, *Hidden Essex*, Countryside Books, Newbury, 1989
Johnson, W.H., *Essex Tales of Mystery and Murder*, Countryside Books, Newbury, 2001
Jones, Adrian, *The Baby Belsham Mystery*, Essex Police History Notebook No. 44, Chelmsford, undated
Jones, Richard Glyn (ed.), *Killer Couples*, W.H.Allen & Co Inc Star Books, London, 1989
Jones, Steve, *Wicked London*, Wicked Publications, Nottingham, 1989
Kay, F. George, *Lady of the Sun (The Life and Times of Alice Perrers)*, Frederick Muller Ltd, London, 1966
Kent, Sylvia, *Folklore of Essex*, Tempus Publishing, Stroud, 2005
Le Lievre, Audrey, *Miss Willmott of Warley Place*, Faber & Faber, London, 1980
Maple, Eric, *The Dark World of Witches*, Robert Hale, London, 1962
Marlow, Joyce (ed.), *Votes for Women*, Virago Press, London, 2000
Marsden, Walter, *Resting Places in East Anglia*, Ian Henry Publications, Romford, 1987
Matthews, John, *Boadicea*, Firebird Books, Dorset, 1988
Maurier, du Daphne, *Mary Anne*, Companion Book Club, London, 1955
Morgan, Glyn, *Secret Essex*, Ian Henry Publications, Romford, 1982
Mortimer, Ian, *The Perfect King*, Jonathan Cape, London, 2006
Murphy, Beverley A., *Bastard Prince*, Sutton Publishing, Stroud, 2001
Neale, Kenneth, *Essex in History*, Phillimore & Co Ltd., Chichester, 1977
Occomore, D., *Curiosities of Essex*, Ian Henry Publications, Romford, 1984
O'Leary, John G., *The Book of Dagenham*, Borough of Dagenham, Dagenham, 1937
O'Shea, Katharine, *The Uncrowned King of Ireland*, Nonsuch Publishing Ltd, Stroud, 2005
Oxford Dictionary of National Biography
Payne, Jessie, *A Ghost Hunter's Guide to Essex*, Ian Henry Publications, Romford, 1987
Petchey, W.J., *A Prospect of Maldon*, Essex Record Office, 1991
Pile, Stephen, *The Book of Heroic Failures*, Routledge & Kegan Paul Ltd, London, 1979
Pluckwell, George, *Smuggling Villages of North East Essex*, Ian Henry Publications, Romford, 1986
Pollard, Justin, *The Interesting Bits*, John Murray (Publishers), London, 2007
Prescott, H.F.M., *Mary Tudor*, Eyre & Spottiswoode, London, 1952
Priestley, Harold, *Essex Crime and Criminals*, Ian Henry Publications, Romford, 1986
Pugh, Martin, *The Pankhursts*, The Penguin Group, London, 2001
Ryan, Patricia M. *Woodham Walter: A Village History*, Plume Press, Maldon, 1989
Scott, E.V. (compiler), *The Best of Essex*, Egon Publishers, Baldock, 1988

Smith, Graham, *Smuggling in Essex*, Countryside Books, Newbury, 2005
Snellgrove, L.E., *Suffragettes and Votes for Women*, Longmans, Green & Co., London, 1964
Somerset, Anne, *Unnatural Murder*, Orion Books, London, 1997
Spurrier, Felice, *The Maynards of Easton Lodge*, A Five Parishes Publication, Dunmow, 1992
Spurrier, Felice, *Beyond the Forest*, A Five Parishes Publication, Dunmow, 1986
Standley, A.J., *Chelmsford Prison*, at Essex Record Office, unpublished, 1973
Storey, Neil R., *A Grim Almanac of Essex*, Sutton Publishing, Stroud, 2005
Stratmann, Linda, *Essex Murders*, Sutton Publishing, Stroud, 2004
Stubbings, Wendy, *Lost Gardens of Essex*, Ian Henry Publications, Romford, 2002
Times, The, numerous issues
Tomalin, Claire, *The Life and Death of Mary Wollstonecraft*, Weidenfeld & Nicolson, London, 1974
Torry, J. Gilbert, *Chelmsford Prison*, East Anglian Magazine Ltd, Ipswich, 1980
Tuckwell, Tony, *New Hall and its School*, Free Range Publishing, Edinburgh, 2006
Varlow, Sally, *The Lady Penelope*, Andre Deutsch, London, 2007
Walter, John, *Understanding Popular Violence in the English Revolution*, Cambridge University Press, 1999
Vote, The, various issues
Warren, C. Henry, *Essex*, Robert Hale, London, 1950
Weis, Rene, *Criminal Justice, The True Story of Edith Thompson*, Hamish Hamilton Ltd, London, 1988
White, Malcolm, *Saffron Walden's History*, no publisher, 1991
White's Directory of Essex, 1848

Acknowledgements

Of course, there are always a lot of people involved in producing a book like this. There are those that provide background encouragement such as husband Raymond, and supportive friends such as Donna, Kim, Debbi, Deborah, Judith and Pat. Then there are those who support all local history authors – the well-informed staff at the Essex Record Office in Chelmsford, those at Southend Central Library, Grays Library, Chelmsford Library, Ilford Library, the Women's Library in London, the Museum of London and the British Library.

More specifically, a lot of individuals I have encountered along the way, sometimes by fortuitous accident and sometimes as the result of a specific search, have provided unexpected sources of information on one or more of the women I have chosen to include. Others have assisted with the tracking of suitable photographs which has proved a time-consuming, frustrating and sometimes expensive task. Where some attempts to trace and acknowledge copyright have proved unsuccessful, then this has not been for want of trying. Anyone whose copyright has been unintentionally breached should contact the author through the publisher.

While I have probably missed some people out, for which I apologise, I have to mention Footsteps Photos, John Weedy, Ann and Tony Maxwell, Stephen Northfield, Marjorie Gisi, Ron Ower, Phyll Hendy, Linda Green, Pearl Lonsdale and her son, Claire Hooper, Matthew Bemand, Jeremy Dowding, Alan Cox, Hazel Austin and Maggie Smith at the Thurrock Local History Society, Tom Errington, Patrick Lacey, Captain Thomas Robinson, Chris Pond, and authors John Drury, John Clarke, Patrick Denney, Tony Benton and Rene Weis.